IAN
POULTER
The Biography of Britain's Golfing Hero

First published in 2013 by André Deutsch, an imprint of Carlton Books Ltd

Carlton Books Ltd
20 Mortimer Street
London W1T 3JW

A CIP catalogue record for this book is available from the British Library.

ISBN: 978-0-233-00387-0

Printed and bound by CPI Group (UK) Ltd, Croydon, CR0 4YY

IAN POULTER

The Biography of Britain's Golfing Hero

GAVIN NEWSHAM

ANDRE
DEUTSCH

Contents

Introduction

Watch virtually any episode of *X Factor*, or any other reality TV show for that matter, and you'll always see some overly emotional contestant dribbling on about the "journey" they have been on to get to the point in their lives where they now can be judged, ridiculed and humiliated by a sizeable percentage of the British population. Often, of course, it is a journey that has been tweaked, fine-tuned and exaggerated by TV producers to such an extent where even the contestant can't really recognize their part in the whole rollercoaster ride. The "journey" of Ian Poulter, however, is one that needs no such embellishment.

His is a path that few of the world's top professionals have followed to realize their dreams or achieve their goals and in a day and an age where there are now 12-year-old boys playing European Tour golf, the story of just how a teenage football reject without the wherewithal to compete or the opportunity to even work on improving his golf game can leave behind the constraints of the club shop counter and rise to the very top of the professional ranks remains one of sport's most intriguing and engaging anomalies.

Yes, in the world of professional golf where the US collegiate system churns out PGA Tour players with almost indecent frequency, Ian Poulter is wonderfully and refreshingly different, the full English antidote to the ice-white smiles and perma-tans of a largely anonymous collective of golf pros enjoying everything that the high life has to offer.

How he got there is the stuff of legend and in a game where previous few players have ever done anything resembling a job before they slipped on their sponsored golf shoes and stepped on to the Tour, the story of how he endured and then escaped the day-to-day drudgery of working in a non-descript golf club in a provincial town to seek his fortune reads like some modern-day Dick Whittington.

Even his decision to turn professional with a handicap of four is completely out of the ordinary and reveals a young man who knew exactly what he wanted and how something as insignificant as a comparatively poor handicap wasn't going to stand in his way. What is intriguing, though, is that there must be countless other Ian Poulters out there in club shops right now, taking green fees and giving lessons to hapless hackers, week in week out, with a dream of the big time but without a clue as to how to fulfil it. The issue, then, is how you manage to extricate yourself from the routine and the relative job security, and how you actually make it happen.

Which is precisely where Poulter differs from most other sportsmen. Ever since he arrived in the professional game, his has been a career characterized by making things happen. Golf, after all, needed to change (and many would argue it still does). But someone needed to drag the game, kicking and screaming, maybe not into the twenty-first century – these things take time after all – but certainly into somewhere approaching the latter stages of the twentieth century and Poulter, for one, was determined to play his part in that little revolution.

While Poulter's attitude and appearance today are somewhat removed from that of the player who emerged on the European Tour at the turn of the century – he is now a 37-year-old father of four – his place in the game has certainly changed too. As one of the most recognizable golfers on the planet, he is very much a man in demand and, moreover, one with a significant constituency too, via nearly 1.5 million followers, who chart his progress via Twitter.

While he was certainly confident in his own ability back then, he hadn't yet made a name for himself as one of the more flamboyant characters in the professional ranks. Today, of course, he has grown into the role he carved for himself in the game and, mercifully, he has proved to have the golf game to back up all the many statements he makes, be they verbal, sartorial or even tonsorial.

But, put simply, Ian Poulter is perfect for the game of golf and for every fan who follows him on Twitter, there is another who simply cannot abide the way he goes about his business. But it's that division of opinion that Poulter thrives on. In his eyes, there is only one thing worse than being talked about, and that's *not* being talked about.

Of course, sport is an arena and a world that is awash with hype and hyperbole. It is, after all, the very thing that helps to put bums on seats and keeps Sky Sports in business. But you also need heroes. You need those players and participants who have the unique knack of being able to rise to the occasion when it matters most and who can deliver those displays that will leave jaws on the floor and gobs well and truly smacked. Ian Poulter is, undoubtedly, one such performer, and never more so than when it comes to playing in his *raison d'être*, the Ryder Cup.

Take his steely showing at Medinah in 2012, when he almost single-handedly transformed the European team's fortunes on the

Saturday evening, closing out his and Rory McIlroy's fourballs game against Zach Johnson and Jason Dufner by rolling in five astonishing birdies in his final five holes to steal a point for José-Maria Olazábal's team and give them a modicum of hope going into the Sunday singles matches.

Take Poulter out of that team, remove him from the equation, and it's hard to envisage anybody else in that side stepping up and delivering in such an emphatic and miraculous manner. That Europe's improbable victory will go down in the annals of sport as one of the most inspired performances ever witnessed is assured. That Ian Poulter was the driving force and inspiration for it undeniable.

Certainly, the intensity with which he threw himself into what seemed like a battle already lost at Medinah was like something out of an unrealistic Hollywood action movie. With his eyes bulging, fists pumping and a guttural roar greeting every drained putt, Poulter looked every inch the warrior charging into battle, albeit one wielding a putter rather than a sceptre, and wearing a visor rather than a helmet.

It wasn't the first time he had done it. Indeed, his record in the four Ryder Cups he has played in to date shows a player almost without compare in this most compelling of events. With 12 wins, no ties and just three losses in his 15 matches, his 80 per cent winning rate is the highest in history for those golfers who have played 15 or more games in the Ryder Cup. It's an astonishing return.

But Poulter was ever thus and what is fascinating is that every person that you speak to about the player says the same thing, agreeing that while he may not be the most naturally gifted golfer they have ever laid eyes on, the very fact that he had such an inherent and burning belief in his own ability always made him stand out, whether that was on the school playing fields or in the higher echelons of the professional game.

And you need that in sport. You need to possess that unflinching and unwavering conviction that you are every bit as good or even better than your rivals and contemporaries. You need that basic and vital belief. And if you get a little chutzpah too then all well and good.

Of course, there are plenty of sportsmen and women – and very many golfers – who can only seem to find that belief and that motivation through a sports psychologist or a mind coach. But Poulter had never felt the need for one and insists he never will. And while he got slated for his now infamous "Tiger and Me" comments back in 2008, it was a testament to his conviction that he not only rode out that particular storm but gave as good as he got in return. Besides, in many ways he was right. After all, if you don't aspire to be the best and believe you can get there what's the point in teeing it up in the first place?

But at the time of writing, Ian Poulter had yet to win a major championship and time is ticking on. It's the one blot on an otherwise exemplary copybook that has seen him win in almost every year he has been on Tour, as well as become the first Englishman to win two World Golf Championship events. Of course, he is not alone in that respect and many of his Ryder Cup team-mates, from Lee Westwood to Luke Donald to Sergio Garcia, are all in a similar boat too, but it's the key piece of the jigsaw that, rightly or wrongly, will determine whether he's ever considered as one of the game's truly great players.

To his credit, though, Poulter has often said that even if a major doesn't come his way then he will be content to head off into his dotage with his many Ryder Cup memories for company. And anyway, as Colin Montgomerie's recent induction into the World Golf Hall of Fame clearly proved, the absence of one of the four majors on a CV does not preclude you from joining the feted ranks of professional golf's legendary achievers.

Besides, who is to say he won't have won one by the time you read this?

Not Ian Poulter, that's for certain…

Prologue

It's Saturday, January 29, 1999 and Ian Poulter has been roped in to help redecorate the hallway of his girlfriend Katie's parents' house. It's the least he can do, especially after all the help that Katie's folks have given the couple, what with Katie on her nurse's salary and Ian's golf career not exactly taking off.

But as Ian strips back the wallpaper, he pauses, picks up a nearby decorator's pencil and starts writing on the now bare wall, much to Katie's amusement:

29-1-99
Saturday
IAN JAMES POULTER
EUROPEAN TOUR STAR TO BE
"DECORATING IN SPARE TIME WITH STYLE"? XXX
AND KATIE'S HELP

He then completes his message with a typically over-elaborate signature, circling it all with a final flourish before returning to the job in hand. Hours later, the new wallpaper is up and Poulter's premonition, his decorating time capsule if you like, will be gone and almost forgotten…

Chapter 1
From Rag Trade to Riches

@IanJamesPoulter
*Global tour golfer, @ijpdesign Owner. Massive Arsenal fan and
Orlando Magic fan. Love Cars, Most of all love my Family time*

*A Saturday morning, Stevenage Golf Club, 1983. Seven-year-old Ian
Poulter is caddying for his father, Terry, when they reach the par-three
11th hole. It's 140 yards, downhill, with a stiff breeze against, but with
a fourball ahead on the green Terry's forced to wait until the putting
surface is clear before taking his tee shot. With his young son itching to
have a shot, Terry hands him a cut-down three-wood and, confident he
won't reach anywhere near the green, lets young Ian have a go. Without
so much as a practice swing, Ian drills one right out of the middle of
the clubface. As the ball sails through the air, his dad tracks its progress
and starts to worry. Moments later, the ball pitches on the green, before
racing through the back and causing the fourball ahead to take evasive
action. Terry looks at his son, his initial anger giving way to something
approaching paternal pride. "Now go and apologize," he laughs, "because
you nearly killed one of them."*

There can't be many five-year-old boys who take a pride and a
genuine interest in their appearance, yet alone ones that make a point

of keeping their bedroom tidy at all times. But then there weren't many five-year-old boys like Ian James Poulter, especially not in Stevenage in the 1970s.

The second son of Terry and Theresa Poulter, Ian was one of life's little neatniks, even from an early age. Each morning, he would emerge from his bedroom and make his way down the stairs to seek opinion on whether the clothes he had chosen for the day were properly co-ordinated, even if it was just his standard school uniform. At the weekend, meanwhile, he would roll out the swishier, more stylish togs. Maybe a pink shirt with a grey tie. Perhaps some silk Trevira trousers too, as long as Theresa had ironed them properly and not done them with ghastly double pleats.

Fast forward 30 years or so and Ian Poulter, the Hitchin boy made good, is just as bad, if not worse, when it comes to his clothes collection. Now, his obsession with presentation has evolved to the extent that his clothes are all colour-coded in his cavernous walk-in wardrobe, while the coat hangers must always, repeat *always*, face the same way. And woe betide the dry cleaner who returns his trousers with tramlines. "It's the one thing that absolutely drives me crazy," he admits. "They have to be perfect."

Call it pride in your appearance, attention to detail or just plain old OCD, but it was ever thus. Back in Hitchin in the decade that fashion forgot, little Ian Poulter seemed, at times, to be waging a one-boy war against the conservative and the nondescript, against the dull and the dreary. He was always immaculately turned out, always impeccably dressed, but then that's what happens when you have a child that's as fussy about fashion as most kids are about food.

Of course, you could always blame his mum, Theresa. As the manageress of the Stevenage branch of Dorothy Perkins, she knew a thing or two about fashion, keeping her finger on the pulse of what was hot and what was not, and then keeping young Ian in the loop. But if the idea that Poulter's childhood predilection for tailoring and his desire to maintain certain standards suggested a boy who didn't like the things that most boys of his age enjoyed, then nothing could be further from the truth. Why? Because Terry Poulter made sure of that.

Terry was a sports nut. A talented football player in his youth, he had had trials at several clubs as a teenager and then, when he took up golf, he was soon down to a single-figure handicap before he'd even really put his mind to it. But the main love of his life, after his wife Theresa, obviously, was Arsenal Football Club and like any doting dad, he was determined to pass on the Gunners' gene to his offspring; as soon as Ian was old enough to understand, Terry had decided that he would also support Arsenal and by his fifth birthday, little Ian would have the first of what would be countless Arsenal replica shirts.

With his football team decided, Terry had then moved on to his next great passion – golf. As a member of Stevenage Golf Club, he would often take Ian and his older brother Danny down there and let them hit a few balls, maybe buy them a Cola-Cola and a packet of crisps if they were good. But by Christmas 1982 they'd shown enough promise that he presented the boys with a new set of clubs – not each, that was too costly, but a set to share between them. Three decades later, it's safe to say that that present might just have been one of the best investments Terry Poulter has ever made.

Soon, though, Ian would be searching for the various ways and means to improve his game. He would follow his dad round Stevenage Golf Club at the weekend, watching his swing and learning the etiquette. He would take swings with a cut-down three-wood that Terry had had made for him and he would practise his putting on the living-room carpet. He would even begin to assemble folders of instruction articles from golf magazines, cataloguing them so he knew precisely where to go when he needed a certain query answered or problem solved.

It wasn't just a passion for football and golf that Terry, an engineer by trade, had passed on to Ian, though. No, Terry had also imbued in his youngest son a unique and fiercely competitive streak and a refusal to accept losing as something that was part and parcel of playing sport. Not for him the wishy-washy lines of teachers who would tell kids that it wasn't about the winning but all about the taking part. Quite the opposite. For Terry, and therefore for Ian too, it was entirely about the competition; it was all about the winning. "He [Poulter's father] was pretty handy at most sports, and he never particularly liked losing," recalled Ian. "I guess I've got some of that in me. I don't think it's a bad thing to not enjoy losing. He drilled that in me at an early age."

It didn't matter what sport or game Ian Poulter was playing, he simply had to master it and he had to win. Aged two, he had stolen four-year-old Danny's bike and ridden it off, minus stabilizers, without ever having ridden a bike before. Then, aged nine, he had won an adults' pool tournament (and he can still recall just how that tense final frame panned out to this day). Even now, he refuses to yield to his kids whenever he is playing them at games too. It doesn't matter what it is; they're not going to win.

It has always been this way with Ian Poulter. He was a boy and now a man who is genetically programmed not to accept defeat. In fact, he is a person with an abject hatred of losing. As his brother

Danny once told the BBC: "He just wanted to beat everyone. It didn't matter if it was golf or tiddlywinks – he just wanted to beat you."

By the time Poulter had reached Stevenage's Barclay School, the state secondary that sounded much posher than it really was, it had seemed that football and not golf was where his future lay. With his larger-than-average frame and marked composure on the ball, he had quickly been earmarked as an obvious candidate for the school football team. Versatile and quick-witted, Poulter would, in time, become a key member of the Barclay first XI, as one of his PE teachers, Steve Green, explains. "Ian was always quite physically imposing but he could certainly play," he recalls. "He wasn't just some big lad who went around kicking people but he was very competitive and a very talented all-round sportsman. Basketball, cricket, it didn't matter – he just seemed to pick up skills very quickly. It was the same with golf when he took that up."

Merv Smith was Poulter's other PE teacher during his time at Barclay and he agrees that if his former pupil seemed destined to make a career out of any sport it would almost certainly have been football. "He could play anywhere, he really could; in the middle, at the back or upfront as a centre-forward, but he was one of those boys that was everywhere, taking a throw-in on the left wing one minute and then another on the right wing the next."

What was noticeable, even in his early teenage years, was the burning desire to win that he still displays on the golf course to this day. He was assertive, committed and extremely demanding of all of his team-mates too. "Ian was an aggressive player who liked a tackle and liked to win the ball and you can still see that in his character today. He was a winner then and he is now," explains Merv Smith. Occasionally, though, Poulter's competitive nature would get the better of him on the field of play, invariably when one of his team-mates had let him and the side down and he had been forced to pick up the slack. "Sometimes, we would have to pull him to one side and tell him to calm down," adds Smith.

When it came to the academic side of school, however, Poulter was less competitive. It wasn't that he was difficult or unresponsive, it was just that he would rather have been outside kicking or hitting some kind of sphere around. "He was a normal state-educated Stevenage boy," says Steve Green. "But Ian was probably like 99 per cent of boys at school in that he could have achieved much more if he had put his mind to it. But I'm sure if Ian had a choice of doing some English homework or going for a round of golf it wouldn't be a surprise which one he chose. But has it done him any harm? I'll let you be the judge of that."

It's a view backed up by Merv Smith. "Ian was never an academic but he wasn't daft," he insists. "It was just that he liked doing sport and outdoor things. The classroom just didn't turn him on."

Both men, however, agree that even though Poulter could have done better at school, it was almost inevitable that he would go on to make a success of whatever it was he chose to turn his hand to. "Ian was certainly the kind of character that was determined to make the very best of his talent and he's certainly done that," says Smith.

"Sometimes you can just tell the kids that are going to go far," adds Green, "and in Ian there was always something there. Always a real will to win and to succeed."

What was noticeable, at least to Green, was the marked difference in the characters of Ian and his older brother Danny. While Ian was all blood and thunder on the field of play, Danny, two years above him, was decidedly more relaxed. "Danny was different," says Green.

8

"He was much more laid-back and had a entirely different approach to sport. That's not to say he wasn't talented – he was a great golfer – but like many brothers they were just different people."

Poulter's skills on the football field would soon attract the interest of professional clubs. Stevenage had long been a big football town and a rich source of young soccer talent and Poulter would soon be invited to try out at Tottenham Hotspur, the arch enemies of his beloved Arsenal. Thanks, but no thanks came the answer.

The rejection, while disappointing, simply served to make Poulter's mind up about which sport he wanted to pursue and it wasn't going to be football. Besides, in soccer there was always going to be an element of subjectivity, where the opinion of one coach or talent scout might differ wildly to that of another and where you could always be let down by your team-mates when you were depending on them most. There was no such problem in golf: it was you versus the golf course. It was as simple as putting the ball in the hole in the fewest number of shots. Mind you, it was also better for his asthma too.

But while more mainstream sports were catered for at Barclay, the idea that golf would or could ever be an integral part of the PE curriculum there was as far-fetched as it was alien. Twenty-two boys kicking a football around a pitch was one thing, but 22 boys carving golf balls all over the school's property? That was a recipe for disaster, not to mention a Health and Safety headache. "Golf simply wasn't taught at state schools and it isn't really now," adds Steve Green. "It may be in the private sector, but it's not in state schools."

For those boys who did want to play golf the only option was to do so in their own time and at their own expense. Dave Marley was in the year below Poulter at Barclay School and one of a handful of young boys at the secondary who were keen golfers; often their golfing paths would cross in occasional school competitions or some of the countywide schoolboy golf events in Hertfordshire. Though Poulter was flirting with a single-figure handicap by the age of 14, the boys typically played off anywhere between 10 and 15. Certainly, though, Poulter stood out – only not for his golfing ability. "Ian was a good sportsman, a decent footballer, definitely competitive and confident. Dare I say a bit cocky? I don't think he'd disagree with that!" recalls Marley. "He was a good golfer, in the way that kids who had played for enough years when they're young enough tend to be. He certainly wasn't outstanding, though. None of us were. We could all knock it round in 80 on a good day, and 90 on a bad one. There was nothing, at that stage, to suggest that Ian would make it as a professional, let alone one who has enjoyed so much success at such a high level. We were all fans of the game, and probably all fancied a go on the Tour, but it was just kids day-dreaming."

It's something that Poulter himself agrees with, as he explained to *Golf Digest* magazine in June 2010. "If anybody who knew a lot about golf saw my game when I was 18 they never would've said I'd become a great player. I've just been ruthless in my mind and continued to say I'm going to achieve this. Anyone who applies themselves in the right way can achieve anything. You have as much right as anyone."

Dave Marley's interest in golf would evaporate when the delights of student life took hold, but he has still taken a keen interest in the ongoing saga of Ian Poulter's golf career. In fact, it's something that's followed him around the world, as he explains. "When I got to the age of 17 or 18 and started going out on the weekends and then to university, my interest in golf fell off. I would still play a bit – still do – but I had no interest in working on my game. That obviously wasn't the case for Ian. I'd see him from time to time at the driving range when he was an assistant pro, but he was at the selling Mars bars to hackers stage, not lighting up the European Tour.

"I remember seeing him in a pub one time after he'd won a regional pros event – it might have just been an event for assistant pros – and I had a brief chat with him. I congratulated him and asked what was next and he said Tour school. I wished him luck and that was about that.

"I moved to Japan for a few years and was living there when he had his first Tour win. I was surprised, as you would be. And probably a bit envious. But I wasn't altogether shocked. His relatively slow progress as a junior – compared to a lot of people on Tour – has been well documented, but anyone who's played knows that the mental side of the game is huge.

"Ian obviously has great mental strength to cope with the pressures of the game – probably better than a lot of other pros who might have more natural talent. That side of things is really evident in his amazing performances in the Ryder Cup. I've not seen him for years and years but I obviously congratulate him on what he's achieved – a Stevenage boy made good!"

There was, of course, another issue with playing golf – it wasn't cool. Football was fine. It was what the kids played in Stevenage. But golf? That was, well, a bit weird, an old man's sport. But did it bother Poulter? What do you think? "I didn't give a hoot when I was the only kid playing golf at school and the other kids singled me out," he said. "I knew what I wanted to do and what I wanted to be. I haven't given two monkeys what people say."

Of course, you need a thick skin to make it in sport. All too often, critics, commentators and fans alike can be too hasty in offering their opinions, be they informed or otherwise, but those days at Barclay when Poulter was teased about his love of a game that only businessmen and retirees seemed to play were like water off a duck's back to someone as passionate as he.

The only issue with golf, as far as he was concerned, was the cost and while playing at the weekend was all well and good it wasn't right that Terry and Theresa had to put their hands in their pockets every time their youngest son wanted to tee it up. It meant only one thing and, faced with the choice of leaving the clubs at home or finding his own money to pay for his hobby, Poulter, now 13, got a job that also indulged the other fascination in his young life – fashion. Now every Saturday, he would head down to Stevenage's outdoor market and work a shift at a men's fashion stall, selling trendy T-shirts and jeans and also showing a rare aptitude for the job. At the end of each day, he would receive £15 for his troubles, a wage that would soon rise to £25, such was his salesmanship. He even got to stand in for the boss when he was away.

By his mid-teens, Poulter was spending increasing amounts of time on his golf. Whether knocking it round with his dad and his mates at Stevenage Golf Club at the weekend or squeezing in a few holes at twilight, his obsession continued to grow apace. Aged 15, he would begin to go to tournaments and try to blag a ball or two from Seve Ballesteros or Colin Montgomerie (he still has them). He would also attend an exhibition by Nick Faldo in 1991, who, by then, had won four of his six majors. Fresh from back-to-back Green Jackets at Augusta, Faldo would hold the young Poulter spellbound as he speared balls into the distance with his laser-like one-iron. It was at that moment, as another ball arrowed off into the clouds, that Poulter decided that he wanted to be a professional golfer. It was that moment when all the really hard work would begin.

Even at this stage, though, the difference between Poulter and the likes of, say, Tiger Woods and Rory McIlroy couldn't have been more pronounced. These, after all, are golfers who have almost been bred to play the professional game. Woods, famously, once putted a ball on TV's *The Mike Douglas Show* aged just two and then also shot 48 over nine holes round the Cypress Navy course in California a year later. McIlroy, meanwhile, had also been earmarked for golfing greatness at an early age, hitting 40-yard drives almost as soon as he could walk. And here was Poulter, still relatively new to the game but just as determined to make it, even though he had none of the grounding that most other players had benefited from.

But he would not be dissuaded. A year later in 1992, Poulter would join the Jack O'Legs Golf Centre (now known as Chesfield Downs Golf & Country Club), a couple of miles north of Stevenage, as a junior member, although as Keith Bond, the head coach, recalled in 2012, it wasn't as though the club's golfing prayers had been answered when the young Ian Poulter first walked through their doors. "He just wasn't a standout player," he told the *Daily Telegraph*. "But he really believed he would go on to great things. He told everyone at school he was going to be world No.1. He told people here that he was going to win European Tour events. Everyone thought, 'Well, he doesn't know what he's talking about.' But he did. And we didn't."

Members at Jack O'Legs recall a young man whose swing was functional but ultimately quite unremarkable. It was neither classic and smooth, nor was it wild and untamed. But where Poulter did excel was on and around the greens, displaying a rare deft touch and a natural putting stroke that would hold him in good stead not just through his teenage golf but on through his professional career. But what membership now afforded Poulter was easy access to the golf course and the club's practice facilities, something that he would avail himself of as often as he could. It paid rapid dividends too. Within a year, Poulter would win the Club Championship, taking the title at just 17 and earning his own place on the honours board on the clubhouse wall.

But with his handicap stalling at four, he made a decision that, at the time, could either be construed as risky or an act of unparalleled idiocy: he turned professional. It wasn't completely out of the blue, though, as Poulter had seen his brother Danny also pursue a career as a PGA qualified professional and, encouraged by his progress, had decided to give it a go himself. And so what if there were scores of players at Jack O'Legs with better handicaps than him – none of them had the big dreams that Poulter had nor did they possess the gut-busting drive and determination to make them a glorious reality.

But a professional needed a job and as luck would have it there was a junior position going at Jack O'Legs. Initially at least, life in the pro-shop was good fun, even if all they ever seemed to do was fold shirts, something the ever-fastidious Poulter excelled at. There was a rare camaraderie among the junior professionals and no small measure of high jinx when the boss wasn't watching. There would also be some fascinating field trips to be had too – quite literally. Take the 1993 Ryder Cup match at The Belfry in Sutton Coldfield. As the premier team event in professional golf, it was one of those competitions that any golf fan worth their sand wedge couldn't afford to miss, although in Poulter's case it was an event he couldn't really afford to attend either.

Desperate times require desperate measures. Packing up his battered old Ford Fiesta with a camping stove and some canned food – curried beans to be specific – and cheap booze, Poulter and two of his fellow assistants headed north to the Midlands. But without the wherewithal to rent a room in one of the hotels, all of which had suddenly inflated their prices for the week, he and his mates decided to hedge their bets and take a tent. The problem, however, was that even the campsite near The Belfry was full.

Undeterred, the lads cheekily asked the site owner if they could pitch their tent in her back garden and for the tidy sum of just £3 a night she said yes. It was game on. That week, the trio would wake each morning, stiff-necked and a little hung-over, and walk the three miles to The Belfry to watch Bernard Gallacher's Europe take on Tom Watson's United States team. "Three guys in a small, confined space, eating tinned food each night and a few bottles of wine," Poulter would recall. "She [the owner] used to let us go in the house and wash up, and then we would go to sleep and get up in the morning and walk to the golf course."

For Poulter it was heaven on earth (albeit in the West Midlands) as one household name went head to head with another; Ballesteros, Langer, Faldo and Woosnam on one side, Wadkins, Kite, Floyd and one of Poulter's heroes, Payne Stewart, on the other. On the Sunday they were even close at hand to see a bit of Ryder Cup history as Faldo made only the second hole-in-one in the contest at the 189-yard, par-three 14th hole in his singles match against Paul Azinger. "I remember thinking, 'I want a piece of that.' That to me was the turning point. It was… 'Wow!' I had never heard anything like that. Wouldn't it be great to do that myself?"

Chapter 1

Even though Europe eventually lost 15–13, their second successive defeat in the Ryder Cup, Ian Poulter had fallen hook, line and sinker for the magic of the event and that uncomfortable week spent bedding down in a stranger's back garden had nevertheless proved to be one of the most exhilarating of his young life. "That was when I said, 'This is what I want to do. I want to be a pro, I want to do my PGA exams and I want to play. I want to win tournaments on the European Tour and I want to win tournaments around the world.'"

Chapter 2
Sweet, Sweet Nothings

@IanJamesPoulter
If I'm ever happy in defeat that day will be the last day I ever hit a golf ball… I am a bad loser. I've never known a good one.

In many ways, the Mars Bar is the perfect golf snack, at least in the temperate golf climate of the United Kingdom, where the sun hasn't really made an appearance since 1976. Yes, don't let Padraig Harrington or any other fruit fiend golfer fool you that the banana or, worse still, the protein bar is where it's at: it's the Mars Bar, that chunkiest and most satisfying of confectionery delights that ticks all of the boxes when it comes to solid sustenance on the golf course.

Ian Poulter had had a gutful of Mars Bars. Not literally, of course, rather the never-ending succession of them that he had to wearily hand over the counter to the weekend hackers at the golf club. It wasn't just taking the green fees and doling out snacks that was taking its toll, though. There was the stock-taking, shelf-filling and the endless vacuuming of the clubhouse floor. And all for £3.20 an hour. This was hardly the rollercoaster golf lifestyle that Poulter had envisaged when he turned professional.

If you watch professional golf either live at a Tour event or at home on the television, you might assume that here is a sport and a lifestyle that is incomparably glamorous, characterized by first-class travel and five-star accommodation, and where the only headache is just how you're going to get from the hotel to the heliport. But there are only a few players, a very happy few, who can enjoy such luxury.

It's like professional footballers. Precious few of them really earn the kind of money that would make an investment banker blush and for every Wayne Rooney on £250,000 a week there are hundreds in the lower leagues scraping by on little more than the average national wage – and sometimes even less. It's the same in golf, where even those players on the Tours immediately beneath the main PGA and European Tours struggle to make a decent living. Take that down several more levels and you will reach the position of club professional and, below that, assistant professional, a role which is often more about skivvying and servitude than it is about soaring seven-irons and sensational sand saves.

Of course, all youngsters who become golf professionals dream of making it on Tour. It's what they're in the game for. Many are called, though, but few are chosen and while Poulter has often said that his brother, Danny, was the better golfer of the two when they were growing up, it was Ian who possessed that indefinable quality, other than talent and aptitude, that gave him a head start over his contemporaries.

Yet Poulter's dreams of golfing stardom seemed strangled by the drudgery – the reality – of being a young golf professional. Even the money he was getting gave him little or no opportunity to practise, not least because while he could use the range as much as he wanted when his shift was done, his boss at Jack O'Legs (soon to be renamed Chesfield Downs) insisted that he still had to pay green fees every time he wanted to play, just like any other punter.

Even when he did get a chance to get the clubs out it would only be to teach junior golfers at £1 a lesson. And if he wanted to play in a competition, well, then he had to take the day off.

A potted history lesson for the unaware may be in order here. Jack O'Legs, for those who don't know, was Hertfordshire's very own Robin Hood character. A fourteenth-century cave-dwelling giant, he would roam the countryside robbing the rich and then give the loot to the county's poor and needy. The difference between that Jack and the Jack O'Legs that Poulter now found himself working for was that, in Ian Poulter, Jack had also taken to robbing the poor.

With cash scarce, hope low and the future uncertain, Poulter was at a crossroads. Here was a player who had belief and confidence in spades but for one reason or another was being stymied by an inability to improve. He knew he had the talent – or at least he thought he did – but he wasn't getting many opportunities to test it. In 1995, though, Poulter decided to take a day off (unpaid, obviously) and entered The Panshanger Classic, a low-level professional tournament held in Welwyn Garden City, the same town where Nick Faldo was born.

Despite rarely having the chance or the finances to pit himself against his fellow professionals, Poulter found the event and the challenge to his liking and promptly returned home with his first ever trophy. The next day, he took the cup into work and, while he wasn't really expecting the ticker-tape parades that Ben Hogan used to get when he won, he did think there would be at least some pats on the back to be had as he proudly placed the trophy on the pro shop counter to show the members. No sooner had he put the trophy on display, though, than word came from on high to remove it immediately. "It was a kick in the ribs," said Poulter, years later.

At first sight, it may have appeared that such a despotic regime may have had grave consequences for Poulter but, if anything, you could argue that it was the best thing that ever happened to him and his golf career and when Ian learned of a job at nearby Leighton Buzzard Golf Club, it was just the push he needed. Interviewing Poulter for the job was the head professional and now one of the UK's top golf coaches, Lee Scarbrow. "He was a cocky young so-and-so," he says, "but he just had something about him so I decided to take a chance."

There is a story, doubtless apocryphal, that maintains that as Poulter had never played enough competitive golf at Chesfield Downs to acquire a handicap certificate he had to employ a little skullduggery of his own in order to land the job at Leighton Buzzard, a position for which one of the pre-requisites was the possession of a bona fide certificate. The day before his interview, he had slipped into the club secretary's office and amended their records to show that he actually had a handicap of four. The next day, he was offered the job.

Though Poulter's time-keeping was awful, Scarbrow noticed in him not just an almost natural ability in folding the shirts on sale in the club shop – it had been drummed into him by his mum and his days on the market – but a drive and determination so rare that the coach has never seen anything like it in all his years in the sport. There was, it seemed, no debate as to where Poulter was heading and no question that Leighton Buzzard was a mere stepping stone on the way to his final target of European Tour golf. "Right from the start he knew he wanted to be a touring pro," adds Scarbrow. "I remember him playing in his first pro event, an East Region PGA 36-hole tournament. The day before he told us all he was going to win it. I thought: 'Yeah, right, Ian,' but, you know what, he did just that. It was impressive that he shot 66-66 to win, but what was more impressive was that he had a massive asthma attack after that first round, spent the night in hospital and still got up to do the business the next day."

It was little victories like this that made Poulter realize what a successful career in professional golf could really mean. After all, it would take six weeks to earn £1,000 working in the club shop and if he could do it in two days knocking a ball round a golf course then why wouldn't he? In time, he would even try his hand in the States, taking a vacation and paying the $500 entry fee to play on the little-known Central Florida Tour and making his money back in no time at all.

In Lee Scarbrow, though, Poulter found a new boss who not only encouraged and nurtured him but also happened to be one of the best coaches in the business too. It was a situation that suited them perfectly. Scarbrow got the best-folded shirts and sweaters in any of the county's pro shops and one of the best salesmen to go with it, while Poulter, in return, got the opportunity to play regular golf and, crucially, to learn and improve. And so what if he also had to take the Under-10s Pee Wee Club and sell a few more Mars Bars? Life at Leighton Buzzard was different, and wonderfully so.

Though he recognized a latent talent in Poulter's functional swing and a short game that could clearly serve him well, Scarbrow's advice to Poulter would boil down to three short words – believe in yourself. Yes, he could have spent an eternity teaching him all the theories and technicalities but what his protégée needed to be doing at this stage in his career was playing the game, not studying it, especially as the bigger amateur events of junior golf had passed him by, depriving him of some quality competition to measure himself against.

Certainly, Scarbrow's advice struck a chord with Poulter. "I've never come across anyone as competitive as Ian," says Scarbrow. "It didn't matter if it was golf or something else, like go-karting after work. Ian always had to win – and usually did. I've coached guys with better swings, but I've never come across anyone with more belief than Ian. One thing about Ian: whatever he believes in, he gets."

Indeed, it's hard to emphasize just how important Lee Scarbrow was in Poulter's formative golf years. Not only did he arm Poulter with the tools and the mindset to make a real go of the game, but in time, he would also introduce his pupil to another man who would help shape his career, Paul Dunkley. "I had no idea how good he was as a golfer but there were three things about Ian that stood out," he told the *Daily Mail*'s golf correspondent, Derek Lawrenson in 2010. "One was his work ethic, for he has always worked unbelievably hard. Second was his self-belief, and the third was his honesty. I have no doubt that, if he hadn't made it at golf, those qualities mean he would have made it at something."

One man who also got to know the young Ian Poulter was the former Tour professional, Mark Litton. Now a rules official for the European Tour, Litton was attached to Chesfield Downs Golf Club when Poulter was a teenager and the two had played a lot of golf together, often crossing paths at competitions. Now, as Litton tried to forge a career in the professional game on the Challenge Tour, he needed someone to drive him to the airport when he was heading off to foreign climes.

Litton and Poulter made an agreement. If Poulter would act as chauffeur, then Litton would pay him, not in cash but with a dozen new Titleist golf balls instead. For an aspiring pro like Poulter, a player who had all the dreams of the big time but none of the means to help him get there, it seemed like a good deal, not so much for the golf balls (welcome though they were) but also for the information and advice that Litton could give him as he tried to establish himself in the professional game.

The deal done, Poulter's new part-time career as a chauffeur was underway and as he ferried Litton around, first in a beaten-up Vauxhall Astra that died after just three months and then in a Ford Fiesta that wasn't much better, the only issue was whether they would actually reach their destination in one piece. "Let's just say he was a bit of a nutty driver," smiles Litton.

But while Litton may have been less than impressed with Poulter's driving and/or the quality of his transport, what did impress him, like Lee Scarbrow, was the overwhelming desire that seemed to dominate everything that Poulter did. "I really don't think you can ever really tell if someone is going to make it and it's so easy to say 'I always knew so and so would', but he has always had the unbelievable inner faith – which he still obviously has," he explains. "I've known a few good players who would say '*if* I got on Tour, I'll do so and so' but with Ian it was always '*when* I do this' and '*when* I do that', never 'if'."

Having self-belief was one thing – and turning professional off a handicap of four is either supreme confidence or stupidity on the grandest scale – but tootling about in a battered Ford Fiesta on the same roads he had travelled all his life and then playing the same golf courses, week in, week out wasn't really the dream job Poulter had imagined. Still, there were some benefits to being back home rather than blazing a trail across the golfing world and in 1996, while Poulter was busy cutting some rug in a Luton disco, he met a local girl, Katie Gadsden, and the two hit it off immediately. Soon, the couple would buy their first house, a £29,000 maisonette where Katie's salary covered most of the bills as Ian, still "earning buttons", was trying to find a way out of his pro-shop duties and on to the fairways full-time. "I made so little working in the pro shop, all I could do was buy the groceries," he said later.

By 1998, Poulter's pro golf odyssey hadn't reached much further than Hertfordshire. He had tried his luck in qualifying for the European Tour in 1996 and 1997 and come up short, and there was little to suggest the prospect of anything other than the life of a club professional. Sure, it was a good, steady job and you could always get someone else, someone younger and keener, to dole out the tee pegs and Mars Bars, but it wasn't what he wanted.

Try as he might, though, Poulter was finding it difficult to make any significant movement in the right direction and in 1998, he would again try and fail to make it through European Tour qualifying school. There were some positives to take away from the experience though, as thanks to his performance on the low-level Hippo Tour – a circuit for club professionals – where he had won once in seven events and topped the Order of Merit, he was able to take a place on the second-tier Challenge Tour, the feeder circuit for the main European Tour.

Put simply, the Challenge Tour was like a smart price or value range version of its big brother. You always had a fair smattering of familiar names and faces playing on it and the locations of the events seemed, on the face of it, to be far-flung and exotic but that's where the similarity ended. Despite the perilous nature of life on the Challenge Tour, however, there was still no shortage of takers willing to step forward and try their luck. It was understandable really. This, after all, was a stepping stone to the big time, a golden ticket for those players who had their eyes on the Taste The Difference European Tour.

Thanks to the generosity of friends, family and a few of the members at Leighton Buzzard, Poulter set off on his Challenge Tour adventure with a fighting fund that may have taken care of him for a few weeks but not much more. One such benefactor was Andy Day, who invested £1,500 of his own money in Poulter's pro dream. Indeed, it's a measure of just how grateful Poulter was, and is, that even today, 15 years on, he still invites Day over to join him at the Masters each year, picking up the tab for the entire trip.

The Challenge Tour would take Poulter to some weird and wonderful places and the kind of golf courses he had never even heard of, yet alone played. Beginning his campaign in Nairobi, Kenya, where he missed the cut in the Tusker Kenya Open, Poulter would travel back to Spain for the marvellously-named Telepizza Challenge. Here he walked away with his first cheque, but the princely sum of €645 wouldn't even cover his expenses for the week.

A couple of weeks later, however, he found himself back in Africa, this time in Abidjan on the Ivory Coast, where, improbably given his first showings on the Challenge Tour, he claimed a two-stroke win in the 18th Open de Côte d'Ivoire. It had been a nerveless display from Poulter in the kind of searing heat that you didn't get very often back in Milton Keynes, especially in April. With a two-shot lead going into the final round, Poulter had stood firm when pressed by the likes of the French duo of Sebastien Delagrange and Marc Pendaries and the Welshman David Park,

who finished with a 69, and Poulter's prize, a winner's cheque for
€11,370 was more than he got in a whole year back at Leighton
Buzzard. "I'm absolutely delighted," said the 23-year-old after
his maiden Challenge Tour win. "This is my first big win as a
professional. I've won on the Hippo Tour, but this means a lot to
me. Now the target is to get my Tour card."

Of all the events to win on the Challenge Tour, moreover, the
Open de Côte d'Ivoire seemed to be the one to win for those players
intent on graduating to the main Tour. In each of the previous three
seasons, for instance, the tournament winners – Massimo Florioli of
Italy, Denmark's Knud Storgaard, and England's John Mellor – had
all gone on to gain their European Tour cards at the end of the year.
The omens, then, seemed promising for Poulter, the future rosy.

But if Poulter thought that such an auspicious beginning would
turn into a procession of glorious victories across the world, he was
wrong. Indeed, in the next 17 events he would miss 11 cuts and
missed cuts meant no money. That said, the win would get him
on the radar of some European Tour events and he would play
(and miss the cut) in both the West of Ireland Golf Classic and the
Scottish PGA Championship later in 1999.

In early May, meanwhile, Poulter had travelled to Bordeaux for the
Novotel Perrier Open de France, another European Tour competition.
While he didn't have a place in the starting line-up, he was the first
reserve, desperately waiting for a pulled muscle or even a dodgy mussel
to render one of the field incapable of playing. As he waited for news,
chipping and putting on the practice green, he noticed Justin Rose
going through some putting drills and went over to talk to him.

Poulter knew only too well who Rose was but then everybody in
golf seemed to. Famously, Rose had arrived in the world of golf like

a wrecking ball when, at the 1998 Open Championship at Royal Birkdale, and aged just 17, he had holed a miracle pitch from the rough at the 72nd hole for birdie and in doing so claimed the Silver Medal as the event's lowest-scoring amateur player.

Though there was a four-and-a-half year age gap between the pair and they had come into the game from vastly differing routes – Poulter from his own home-made, DIY road and Rose rising through the amateur ranks – the two hit it off instantly. Besides, as far as Poulter was concerned, it didn't matter where you came from, it was where you were at and, more importantly, where you were heading – and in that respect he and Rose were certainly singing from the same hymn sheet.

They would room together to keep the cost down and help spur each other on when things maybe weren't going so well. It was especially important for Rose who, having turned professional after his Open exploits at Royal Birkdale, promptly missed the cut in each of his first 21 events on the European Tour. The drop down to the Challenge Tour, then, was the ideal way to rebuild his crumbling confidence and, for that matter, his professional career too. In Ian Poulter, he had found a kindred spirit, a mate who would help him out whenever he needed it. "I think that was an important part of me improving as a player, kind of learning to enjoy myself as well, out on Tour," says Rose. "Yes, I think that was a key period where I felt like, you know, for example, Poulter, the music going on, blaring in the room, that sort of thing, which was something that I wouldn't necessarily have done, and it was quite an insightful period for me, I thought. I actually learned a lot from that. And obviously his confidence, as well."

Fourteen years on and the bond has grown, the friendship strengthened and at the Omega Mission Hills World Cup event in China in 2007, Poulter explained just what had impressed him about Rose and his attitude. "You could see Justin's potential in how he had played, certainly in that Open [in 1998] in the rounds that he put together at the time," he explained. "You know, Justin was going through a tough period, but to see somebody with the will and determination to keep pressing on and keep working on his game; he knew deep down inside that if he kept working that he would be where he is today. And, you know, that's good to see in people when they never, ever, ever give up, and you need that. It would be very easy for someone at that age to just crumble, and Justin hasn't done that."

At the end of the Challenge Tour season, Poulter had played in 20 events and earned a little over €21,000. It could have been more, too, had Poulter not tripped over his golf bag as he was leaving the BIL Luxembourg Open in May and damaged the ligaments and tendons in his ankle. But it had, in the main, been a positive, if costly, experience for the 23-year-old.

Whichever currency you counted it in, though, it still wasn't great, especially as over half of that total had come from the victory on the Ivory Coast and he also had to find the money for everything else, from flights to accommodation to subsistence. More importantly, Poulter's total was still around €10,000 short of 15th place, the last position in the end-of-year money list that guaranteed golfers an automatic card in the main European Tour for the following season.

All of which meant that Poulter would have to endure another nerve-jangling trip to the hell of Qualifying School at San Roque in Sotogrande, Spain. It's an experience unlike any other in professional golf. No private jet or hefty appearance fees for the players who make the trip to Q-School. Instead, there's just ceaseless, creeping pressure and the constant nagging thought that a missed putt here or a duffed chip there can mean the difference between a pot of gold at the end of the rainbow or no pot to you know what in.

First contested in 1976, the European Tour's Q-School is golf's ultimate pressure cooker, a tournament where careers are launched and trashed in equal measure. As a test of golf, the roll call of winners and players who have graduated reads like a who's who of the sport: Ian Woosnam (1977, 1978, 1979), Sandy Lyle (1977), José-Maria Olazábal (1985), Colin Montgomerie (1987), Vijay Singh (1988), Lee Westwood (1993) and Padraig Harrington (1995) to name but a handful. But while it has bred some of the game's true greats, it has also garnered a reputation as a graveyard for golfers too.

Billy Foster, who has caddied for everyone from Seve Ballesteros and Sergio Garcia to Darren Clarke and Lee Westwood, has been at players' sides many times through the final stage of qualifying. "It's the ultimate pressure cooker," he says. "I've been fortunate to have been in the last group at the Masters, the Open Championship and a lot of Ryder Cups, but the pressure at Q-School is right up there with all of them. If you miss a cut at an event on the Tour you've always got next week to make amends. If you make a mess of Q-School you've got to wait another year. If anything, it's tougher trying to come through Q-School than it is trying to win a Tour event. It's all or nothing, simple as that."

The secret, then, is how you deal with the pressure and you would think that after three previous appearances at Q-School – three *failed* appearances – Ian Poulter now possessed the know-how to negotiate the many pitfalls of the event. Other players may have been beset by doubts and crippled by the fear of another failure. But not Poulter.

After six gruelling rounds of golf, Poulter reached the final hole of his final round with a Tour card firmly in his sights. But then the enormity of what he might be about to achieve hit him just as he was hitting his tee shot. Needing a par – and nothing worse – to win his playing rights, he skewed his drive headlong into the trees, leaving him with an almost impossible shot to reach the green. Undeterred, he bravely pulled out his two-iron and in a defiant flash hit it low and true under the hanging branches of the trees obscuring his view and watched as it came to rest at the back of the green. A cool two-putt later and Poulter's par would see him take 23rd place in the final reckoning, comfortably inside the all-important top 30 places, and giving him his European Tour card for 2000.

Three times Poulter had tried to make it through qualifying in a bid to win his Tour card and three times he had come back home with a heavy heart and a huge dent in his bank balance. But now, at his fourth attempt, he had made it through to the Promised Land of the European Tour, where the Westwoods and the Montgomeries played, and where the living was easy. And so too, for that matter, had his mate Justin Rose, 19 places ahead of him in fourth.

Now, as Poulter left the relative penury of the Challenge Tour behind, he could reflect on a job not just well done but one that, in all likelihood, looked in real danger of never quite coming off. But no longer would there be shared rooms and budget diners, no longer would there be hitched rides and hand-me-down clubs. No longer would there be tiny cheques that weren't worth turning up for.

More importantly, Ian Poulter was no longer a "European Tour Golfer To Be".

Chapter 3
Bring on the Big Time

@IanJamesPoulter
Time for an afternoon snooze I think. My brain hurts. That's not easy as I don't have a lot to hurt.

Mums, eh? You have to love them. Look at Ian Poulter's mother, Theresa. Not only did she teach him everything about the inner workings of the fashion retail world and the finer points of folding a sweater, but she's also his number one fan. Who else would stop ironing in order to call up Sky Sports to complain that her son wasn't getting enough airtime during a tournament and then have her complaint read out by the apologetic commentators?

Yes, for all his exploits on the golf course, Poulter's family have always been resolutely behind him as he's sought to make his name in the game. Whether it's dad Terry tweeting every last detail of each putt made or missed, his mum berating broadcasters or Danny giving him a little brotherly advice here and there, it's the kind of tight-knit support network you need pulling for you and the sort of unwavering backing that can make a real difference when you need it most.

Theresa Poulter always knew that Ian had something about him. "Ian's self-belief didn't come overnight," she told *The Times*. "He always had it. I don't think we ever told the boys they were really that good. I think we just complimented them when they did something good. They were never criticised when they lost. My role was to be there when he didn't win and give him a shoulder to cry on, I suppose." Well, that and call Sky Sports to complain, obviously.

Though he was confident, sometimes verging on the cocksure, Poulter's new life as a bona fide European Tour professional had started impressively and the supposed step up in standard he may have expected hadn't really affected him. Within four events he had already earned three times the amount he would have earned in a year back at Leighton Buzzard. Even when he hit his first stumbling block, a missed cut – his first – at the Brazil Rio de Janeiro 500 Years Open, he rectified things immediately, taking a tie for third at the next week's event in São Paolo.

Poulter was playing anywhere and everywhere, from Brazil to Qatar and from Malaysia to Madeira. For the younger players, like Poulter, and the ones yet to be burdened with mortgages or challenged by the demands of young children, the European Tour must have seemed like one giant global playground and certainly Poulter threw himself headlong into the experience.

But not everybody approached the Tour schedule with quite the same vigour. At many events, like the Moroccan Open Méditel in April 2000, where Poulter claimed his highest finish to date – a tie for second – the field contained all the usual faces that he was now accustomed to seeing week in, week out, but still none of the big name players like Darren Clarke, Lee Westwood and Colin Montgomerie that he really wanted to pit himself against. Maybe it was the relatively low prize pot that kept them away or just another tournament they could have done without, but for Poulter it was an interesting lesson in how to ration yourself in order to ensure bigger and better rewards at some of the more prestigious events on Tour.

The perfect example of this came when the Tour moved back to Western Europe. With shorter flight times, less inconvenience and, generally speaking, larger purses, it was noticeable how many of the established and higher ranking professionals now decided to play. But it was also clear just how much more difficult it was to keep pace with the field. In other words, things just got serious.

At the European Tour's flagship event, the Volvo PGA Championship, at a soggy Wentworth, all of the Tour's A-list turned out – even Seve Ballesteros made an appearance. Lured in by a prize fund of nearly €2.5 million, Poulter soon found that when the going got tough, the tough certainly got going on the Tour. A cursory glance at the leaderboard come the end of Sunday showed Poulter just what he was now up against. First was Colin Montgomerie (winning a record third consecutive PGA Championship), second was Darren Clarke, third was Scotland's Ryder Cup player Andrew Coltart, fourth was another Ryder Cup star Lee Westwood and fifth was the hottest young player in world golf and the man who so nearly edged out Tiger Woods in the 1999 US PGA Championship at Medinah, Spain's Sergio Garcia. And how did Ian Poulter do? Well, he laboured badly around the West Course, coming home with a first-round 77 and a follow-up 81 to miss the cut – and all that money – by 12 shots.

The missed cut at Wentworth would signal the start of a dire run of form for the young Englishman and in the next five events he would only figure in the money just once, a tie for 14th at the Compaq European Grand Prix at the Forest of Arden, momentarily punctuating the gloom. At all the big events on the Tour – the

Murphy's Irish Open, the Smurfit European Open and the Standard Life at Loch Lomond – Poulter's form had simply deserted him. Suddenly, the heady days of Brazil and Morocco seemed further away than ever.

It was a run of form that would not only test Poulter's resolve and reveal just how he could deal with the bad times, as well as the good, but also scupper any chance of automatic entry in to the Open Championship at St Andrews. Having a Tour card was one thing but it didn't always mean guaranteed entry into events, especially the bigger ones.

Playing on the Old Course at St Andrews was another of those golfing rites of passage that had passed Poulter by, but the idea that he might now miss the Open Championship there, especially as he was a member of the European Tour, seemed to stir him into action. But the odds weren't great. There were only 156 places in the field for the Open and 100 of those had already been filled by better-ranked players, tournament winners and former champions. For Poulter to qualify, then, he would have to enter the qualifying competition and battle it out against 2,349 other players for one of the remaining 56 places.

The weekend before the Open began, he had driven up to Ladybank, the picturesque golf club 10 miles or so west of St Andrews to take part in final qualifying. It would be a tough two days and 36 brutish holes, but Poulter, despite his recent travails, would prevail. With his place in the starting line-up guaranteed and his first crack at the Claret Jug, he wasted no time in driving down the A91 and straight into St Andrews, just to see what all the fuss was about. Once there, he parked up, right next to the 17th green, the famous Road Hole, and, surveying the scene, crept gingerly on to the putting surface. It was a golf course unlike anything he had ever seen before and one that, in time, would become his favourite of all. "I was like, 'What is this?'" he recalled in 2010. "The greens didn't look like greens to me, they looked like short fairway."

In one mesmerizing moment, Ian Poulter had fallen head over heels in love with St Andrews and the Old Course, just as so many other golfers had across the centuries. It was like Bobby Jones himself had said when he played there: "The more I studied the Old Course, the more I loved it; and the more I loved it, the more I studied it."

But the St Andrews experience was about to get even more memorable. On the first day of the Championship, as the crowds swarmed into town and around the course, Poulter headed off to the range to hit some balls ahead of his opening round. As he limbered up, he noticed an elderly guy knocking balls next to him. He looked familiar, *very* familiar. Then it clicked – it was Sam Snead. Winner of the Open in 1946 and of six other majors, Snead, now 88 years old, was in town to play in the four-hole warm-up tourney, the Champions Trophy, along with the likes of Jack Nicklaus and Arnold Palmer, and here he was knocking up next to Poulter. "That gave me goosebumps," he said later. "Arnie, Jack and a whole group of legends were playing the Champions Trophy that year. I just sat in the clubhouse and watched them all play the four-hole loop."

On the course, the highlight of Poulter's week would be a second-round 69, a score good enough to help him inch past the cut mark and guarantee him a weekend at the Home of Golf. But all the talk that week would be of another 24-year-old competitor, the American Tiger Woods, who would win the Claret Jug with the kind of mastery that nobody had seen since the heyday of Nicklaus. Already one of the most successful players of all time, as well as one of the famous sportsmen on the planet, Woods' performance, just 35 days after winning the US Open at Pebble Beach by a bewildering 15 shots, was nothing short of miraculous as he shot four rounds in the 60s, made just three bogeys and avoided each and every one of the 112 bunkers on the Old Course. His final total of 19-under par, meanwhile, not only took him to an eight-shot victory over Thomas Bjorn and Ernie Els in a very distant second, but also completed his first career Grand Slam of major titles, a mere two years earlier than the mighty Jack Nicklaus.

While Woods was a one-off, a golfing freak in the nicest possible sense of the word, the manner, size and scale of his victory must have been of some concern to Poulter, not least because it highlighted the gulf between him and the very best in the business. Still, it was only his first Open and the experience, from qualifying to making the cut and coming down the 18th on Sunday, had been invaluable. And so what if he had come 64th and finished 22 shots behind the winner? He'd met Sam Snead and that was worth the trip alone.

The Open experience would prove to be a turning point in a season that had been in danger of derailing. In his remaining nine events, Poulter would suffer just two more missed cuts and as he headed into his penultimate event, the Italian Open in Sardinia, he was showing flashes of brilliance, a 68 here or a 67 there, but no real consistent streak of form that would take him into the higher echelons of the final leaderboards, no four-round runs to take him to the top.

But all that would change in the micro-climate of Is Molas. For four days in late October, Poulter's golf came together in beautiful and devastating fashion. Finally, there were 72 holes where the potential he had shown intermittently through the year came to glorious fruition. Four rounds in the 60s where everything seemed to click. And four rounds that would land him his maiden Tour title.

And it wasn't about the money, although an oversized cheque for €166,660 was always going to be most welcome. It was the fact that he had won an event on the European Tour and, as a consequence, guaranteed his card for the following year in the process, that had really counted. Not that he'd ever really doubted it, obviously.

If there was any doubt about just what an impressive debut season Poulter had enjoyed on the European Tour, it was extinguished when the Tour announced the 24-year-old as the Sir Henry Cotton Rookie of the Year for 2000, an award named after the man who, in a sweet coincidence, also designed the Is Molas course on which Poulter had won the Italian Open. But this wasn't any old gong. This was a big deal, as the roll call of previous winners clearly showed; Jacklin, Oosterhuis, Torrance, Faldo, Lyle, Olazábal, Montgomerie, Bjorn, Garcia – anybody who was anybody on the European Tour had got their hands on the award and in Ian James Poulter they had a new winner and one who was determined to outdo every single one of them.

The opening months of any European Tour season are always fascinating to watch, not because they throw up some interesting results (though they often do) but because the location of the events that are played stretch the definition of a 'European' Tour event beyond all recognition. The European Tour ceased being 'European' many years ago, and the nature of professional golf today means that you can just as likely have a European Tour winner in Timbuktu as in Turin or Telford.

A look at Poulter's schedule of early 2001 shows a golfer who was clearly keen to cram in as many competitions as possible. It was very much a case of 'have clubs, will travel'. From mid-January onwards, Poulter racked up the air miles relentlessly. From Bangkok to Johannesburg, on to Perth and then Sydney, before swinging through the Middle East with a customary stop-off in Dubai and Qatar, his breakneck schedule was clearly one designed by an ambitious young player, yet to be weighed down by any of the attendant responsibilities that older players laboured under.

But he was young, energetic and nearly always good to go, as his win at the Moroccan Open in Rabat in mid-April showed. It was also a clear demonstration of just how comfortable Poulter felt as a front-runner too. Having shot the lowest round of the day – a 67 – in the second round, he had held off the concerted efforts of England's David Lynn and Australia's Peter Lonard to record a comfortable two-shot victory.

The win and the €106,506 first prize would propel Poulter not just up the Order of Merit but also into sixth place in the qualification table for the European Ryder Cup team for the match against the United States at the end of September. This was strange, but brilliantly so, and though he had started the season with clear goals and targets, one of them hadn't been making the Ryder Cup team. This was only his second season on Tour, after all. Now, though, he found himself very much in the reckoning for Sam Torrance's team at The Belfry. He was even above Colin Montgomerie, Bernhard Langer and Sergio Garcia in the standings.

But it would be something of a false dawn. In the next five tournaments, Poulter would make just one cut, at the Algarve Open, and while it may have seemed like he had the rest of the season ahead of him to make up the difference, this would be a run that would, in time, put pay to those dreams of Ryder Cup glory.

Any chance he did have of qualifying for the Ryder Cup finally disintegrated at the BMW International in Munich, the last event where qualifying points could be picked up. On a course set up for low scoring – the eventual winner John Daly opened up with rounds of 63 and 64, for instance – Poulter found himself unable to produce the requisite fireworks he needed. But though he had missed the cut – his eighth of the season – he decided against heading home or staying behind to watch the conclusion of the tournament (something golfers rarely do when they've missed the cut). Instead, he spent Saturday night at Munich's famous Olympic Stadium, watching the England football team demolish the old enemy Germany 5–1 in their World Cup qualifying group match. It was just the tonic for a disappointing week and proof indeed that even when golf decides to kick you in the teeth there were always some nice fringe benefits to take your mind off the day job.

But the joy of seeing England win would soon be replaced by despair, anguish and fear. As Poulter geared up for his second crack at one of the lucrative World Golf Championship events, the American Express Championship at St Louis' Bellerive Country Club, news broke of something that suddenly rendered the game of golf absolutely irrelevant. On Tuesday, September 11, 2001, two planes hijacked by terrorists and flown murderously into New York's World Trade Center had seen nearly 3,000 innocent people die, with another plane being flown into The Pentagon and a further hijacked jet crash-landing in a field in rural Pennsylvania. Panic paralysed the planet and with the world facing a new terror and talk of war and retribution filling the corridors of power, something so flimsy and inconsequential as a golf contest suddenly became the last thing on anyone's mind.

The decision to cancel the WGC was taken almost immediately and as the attacks had taken place just 17 days before the 34th Ryder Cup was due to begin at The Belfry, the decision to postpone that event for 12 months would follow soon afterwards. Even the European team captain Sam Torrance, a man who had given his life to the game, conceded that "golf is nothing, nothing". He was right, of course, but then he usually was.

It was a view backed up by his opposite number, Curtis Strange, who explained why his team could no longer make the trip to the United Kingdom. "They're human," he said. "They want to be with their families, just like everyone else. They're talking to their children, trying to reassure them that we're not going to war. They were also very consistent in saying we really can't think much about golf right now. It's a tough situation all round."

Yes, in the grand scheme of things, a little game like golf didn't matter a jot. Indeed, amid the horror and the futility of that darkest of days, everything else seemed insignificant and irrelevant.

With professional players the world over suddenly thinking twice about travelling, golf seemed to be on hold and Ian Poulter would not return to competitive action until nearly a month after the events of 9/11, as he teed it up at the Linde German Masters in Cologne. It seemed strange to be playing golf again. Weird that something so ultimately pointless as a game like this could and should still be of any importance to anyone, but life had to go on. A finish of tied-15th, meanwhile, would only be welcome because it was the first cut he had made since the Volvo Scandinavian Masters at the beginning of August.

Poulter's poor form in the latter half of the year had seen him slide down to 27th in the Order of Merit, some way adrift of the top 15 placing that would guarantee him automatic entry to all four major championships in 2002. "My goals have changed from last year," he said. "I've gone from being a rookie to trying to get into the top 15 to qualify for the majors next year. Winning the rookie title opened a few doors and hopefully finishing in the top 15 will open a few more… I think my game is back in shape now."

It had helped that he also managed a spot of R & R with his brother – a four-day break in the Algarve – before he had headed back to Sardinia to defend his title at Is Molas. With the younger brother keen to recapture some form and Danny preparing for the qualifying stages in his bid to win Tour status, it would prove to be the ideal holiday for the pair. It worked wonders too, at least for Ian, as he put up a spirited defence in Sardinia, finishing in a tie for third place.

While he may have missed out on the Ryder Cup and his bid to reach the top 15 in the Order of Merit – he would end in 24th place – Poulter's progress was simply undeniable. He had won again, his stroke average was lower than the previous year and his bank balance even healthier.

But the winter break, while welcome, would stop Poulter in his tracks. Come the new season, the top tens and high finishes he had been seeking, and doubtless expecting, were rarer than a Ferrari 250 GTO. It was a sluggish and sloppy start to the season, characterized by missed cuts and some awfully patchy performances that saw him return just two sub-70 rounds from his first 28 on Tour in 2002. In fact, Poulter would not register his first strong finish until June's Victor Chandler British Masters at Woburn – the club that would soon hire him as their Touring Professional – where he would shoot four rounds in the 60s but still lost out by a single stroke to his friend, Justin Rose. After winning the Dunhill Championship in Johannesburg, South Africa, in mid-January, Rose's second title of the season had seen him bag another high-profile win. The consolation for Poulter was that in coming in as runner-up he had just landed the biggest cheque of his career, earning a few cents short of €220,000 for his week's work.

At the presentation after the round, both men sat by the green in their identikit TaylorMade caps and white adidas polo shirts and laughed like drains. It was strange, surreal even, that just a few years earlier the two novice professionals were sharing rooms as they slogged their way round the circuit trying to eke out a living. Now they were battling it out at the top of the leaderboard in some of the European Tour's biggest events.

It was also testament to the impact that Poulter had had on the European Tour that even Sam Torrance, the European Ryder Cup captain, was now considering him for a place in his team. The event had been postponed for 12 months following the atrocities of 9/11 but now, having had an extra year to prepare for the contest, Torrance's team – the original team for the match in 2001 – seemed to be afflicted by all manner of injuries and ailments. Colin Montgomerie was nursing a bad back, Thomas Bjorn was suffering badly with shin splints and Lee Westwood had a bad case of recurring pins and needles.

While it looked bad for Torrance and his ailing troops, it seemed very promising for Ian Poulter, who was placed on standby, ready to fill in, should one of the trio fail to pull through. Sadly for the young Englishman, all three players would recover in time to play their part in another memorable and tear-jerking victory as Paul McGinley sank the winning putt at the 18th to make Sam Torrance a Ryder Cup winner as player and captain.

Even though he may not have made the team, the fact that Poulter was now being mooted as a Ryder Cup player was the clearest indication of just how far he had come in the game. Less than 10 years previously, he had been sleeping in a tent in someone's back garden and then walking to The Belfry just to watch the event from behind the ropes. Now, he was dangerously close to getting the other side of them – and it wouldn't be long before he was doing just that.

Maybe being in contention for a last-minute Ryder Cup berth was the boost Poulter needed, because a largely disappointing season was rounded off in style when he returned for the Italian Open – held in 2002 at the Olgiata Golf Club, near Rome. A sparkling first-round 61 set him on course for an eventual two-shot victory over Scotland's Paul Lawrie, in a tournament shortened by rain.

By 2003, Poulter was already in the habit of making plans for the new season and setting himself often ambitious targets. The three Tour titles he had already won had imbued him with the belief that he had the necessary talent and temperament to compete at the highest level, but the idea that he could be happy with claiming just one win a year was anathema to him, even if many other players on Tour would be more than satisfied with such a record. This time, Poulter had set his sights on winning at least two tournaments and securing a significant rise up the world rankings.

But he was also very much on the radar of the sports media now too, and not just because of his results on the golf course. Though his performances had, inevitably, brought him to the attention of the golf media, so too had his appearance which, in the world of golf, was a little out of the ordinary.

Not everybody took to it. The *Daily Telegraph*'s website, for example, was unusually harsh. There, under the headline, "The Worst

Dressed Men and Women in Sport" – alongside images of Serena Williams' denim tennis skirt, David Beckham's sarong, Dennis Rodman's bra top and the technicolour rainbow yawn that was John Daly's tournament trousers – was not one but four pictures of Ian Poulter, detailing just why he merited inclusion in the list.

It wasn't really fair, especially as there were innumerable players in the game who barely paused for thought when they threw their clothes on in the morning; at least Poulter made an effort. Still, his predilection for trying new and different looks was already beginning to garner some media attention and not all of it was as spiteful as the *Telegraph*'s assessment.

But then it doesn't take a great deal to stand out in certain sports. In tennis, all you have to do is kick the ball back to the ballboy and you're immediately labelled as one of the game's "characters". Similarly, in snooker all you need is a nickname to get you noticed. Look at Mark "The Jester from Leicester" Selby. Here is a player who looks as if he's never smiled in his entire life, let along entertained anybody in a comic fashion, but because his hometown happens to rhyme with "jester" his (undeserved) reputation as one of the game's jokers always precedes him.

In golf, there are also ample opportunities for self-promotion and Ian Poulter was fast becoming a past master in the pursuit. He had come a long way, too. If you study the photographs from the early years of Poulter's professional career you can see just how massively his image has changed. Back then, quite understandably, he was a picture of conservatism, another golfer that you wouldn't be able to pick out from a line-up of players arrested for crimes against fashion. The polo shirts were baggy, the pleated trousers even baggier and the haircut eminently sensible.

You couldn't blame him really. When you're new on Tour, it's easier just to try and fit in than to rock the boat, simpler to stay out of the way rather than draw attention to yourself. But by 2003, Poulter had already amassed three years of experience in the top ranks, three years where he had learned, sussing everything out and seeing where you could have a little fun.

In 2003, though, strange things were beginning to happen with Poulter's image, not so much with the clothes, which, for the most part, remained safe and surprisingly unstylish, but with what was going on in and, more pertinently, *on* his head. One minute he looked like he had just returned from an audition for an eighties Kajagoogoo tribute band, the next it seemed as if he'd had an unfortunate encounter with a vat of peroxide. Had he been older you could have perhaps put it down to a mid-life crisis, but he was only 27.

At the Nissan Irish Open at Portmarnock, Dublin, in July, Poulter unveiled a bold and brave new hairstyle that was blond and voluminous underneath (in much the same way Colin Montgomerie's was when he first started playing on Tour), but – and here's the key difference – also had huge red streaks running through it, including one right across the front of his head. Later, Poulter would defend his new "style", maintaining that it was a tribute to his beloved Arsenal, although it looked more like a porcupine that had been involved in a road traffic accident with the Gunners' team coach. A week or so later at the Nordic Open, meanwhile, the red swathes had given way to black. Perhaps the change of colour had been designed to reflect his mood? Maybe it was a nod to some distant Goth phase he had been through? Whatever it was, it still wasn't a good look.

But the haircut he revealed at the Dunhill Links Championship that autumn took not just the biscuit but the entire barrel. Truly, it was a style designed by the devil and for a man who prides himself on his appearance and is now seen as one of the Tour's premier trendsetters, the mere mention of it, yet alone seeing it in all its hideous majesty, must make him recoil. Where to start? Well, think of the hair of a Lego man that's been dipped repeatedly in Lurpak butter.

Of course, it didn't help that Poulter was still wearing golf caps that covered all his head, which as any golfer knows, can play havoc with your hair after a long and sweaty round. In time, of course, he would swap the baseball-style cap for the comfort and slightly more hair-friendly visor, as preferred by the Tom Kites, Colin Montgomeries and Luke Donalds of the world, but for now, his already questionable hairstyles were in danger of looking far worse.

In the staid world of professional golf, where a misplaced cough on an opponent's backswing can result in an international incident and where failure to adhere to certain standards of etiquette is tantamount to trampling on the grave of Bobby Jones, it can be difficult to really express your true character. But after three years on Tour where he had won three titles and taken over €2 million in prize money alone, it was clear that Poulter was now beginning to enjoy himself in the Tour ranks, as if his fantastic success had brought with it its own kind of acceptance and acclaim.

Already, though, there seemed to be a division appearing between those who liked Poulter's attitude and the sense of fun he brought to the game and those who viewed him with the same kind of suspicion as one might view a hooded lad on a street corner late at night. But Poulter wasn't up to no good, not really. He was just trying to liven things up a little. Besides, he knew on which side his bread was buttered and there was nothing he was going to do to jeopardize the opportunity he had carved for himself in professional golf.

After those distant days of Hoovering the clubhouse floor and getting £3.20 an hour, the sport was now giving him the lifestyle he had craved but it seemed, at times, as if the lifestyle and the day job were occasionally incompatible. Going into the Wales Open at Celtic Manor in late May, for instance, there was no suggestion that Poulter was in any kind of shape to mount a decent challenge. Six missed cuts from 12 events – including another at his least favourite course, Wentworth at the Volvo PGA Championship – and less than €45,000 banked suggested that his initial targets for the season weren't just ambitious but actually rather unrealistic.

Poulter's growing stature on the Tour hadn't gone unnoticed by the rest of the players. Mind you, it was hard not to notice. At Celtic Manor, for instance, he had turned up in his new Ferrari, parking it underneath the hotel as he went about his day job. Such a conspicuous vehicle, however, was always going to be a target for vandals, although an attack from fellow players wasn't the most likely source.

After a Saturday night out, fellow professionals Mark Roe and David Lynn had returned to the hotel and spotted Poulter's new Ferrari in the parking lot. Lynn looked at Roe and the pair decided to have a little fun. "We got a marker pen and went and sat behind his car because we were going to deface his [rear] number plate, which at the time was 'Ian P'. I don't know which one of us it was, but we sat there for about 10 minutes just looking at it and one of us had the brainwave of turning it into 'TAMPAX'. It was the easiest plate to turn into 'TAMPAX' because it was like, done for you. It just looked absolutely beautiful and you could see him driving home because you don't have a boot on this Ferrari, so you have no reason to go around the back of the car for anything."

The following day, and still blissfully unaware of the newly personalized number plate, Poulter teed off. Several hours later, following a comfortable round of 70, he had closed out a superb three-shot victory. Lynn and Roe, meanwhile, would both miss the cut.

But if the pranksters thought they had got away scot-free they were wrong. Three weeks later at the Diageo Championship at Gleneagles, Lynn would be driving to the golf course from his hotel when he noticed some of the course marshals looking at the front of his car and laughing. When he got out he checked his licence plate only to find that "D LYNN" had been altered, rather creatively, to "DIZZY NOB".

Poulter followed his win at Celtic Manor with a second place at the Danovo British Masters in the Forest of Arden – a finish that saw him take his total winnings from the last two events to over half a million Euros. But this success failed to spark the kind of revival that he may have hoped for. There were more missed cuts at the Diageo at Gleneagles and the European Open at the K Club, while at Sandwich's Royal St. George's in the Open Championship he all but played himself out of contention on the very first day with an ugly 78. Three solid rounds in the low 70s in difficult conditions would show his fighting spirit as he went on to claim a tie for 46th, but there was never any danger that Poulter might trouble the engravers.

All of which made what happened at the Nordic Open all the more surprising. Played at the delightfully-named Simon's Golf Club in Copenhagen, Denmark, the Nordic Open was the first time that a European Tour event had been held in the country and, clearly, it was a tournament to Poulter's liking as three opening rounds of

68, 67 and 65 sent him into Sunday's final round just a single shot behind the leaders, Colin Montgomerie and the home favourite, Soren Hansen.

Playing in the penultimate group, Poulter would take the lead on the eighth hole and maintained his advantage despite a strong challenge from Montgomerie. Making birdies at 11, 12 and 15 and playing a bogey-free round, it was an exemplary exhibition in how to close out a tournament and one that Montgomerie himself would have been proud of. As the Scot played the last, Poulter sat in the scorer's tent, cupping his ears to see if Montgomerie would make the putt that would take him into a play-off. The resultant groan, meanwhile, told him he had not. "It was really another perfect day," he said later. "I got off to a nice start. What can I say? Just kept splitting fairways and hitting it to 15 feet and I knew that 22 or 23 under was going to be a very good total. I thought 66 could be good and thankfully for me Colin missed the putt on the last. I had a chance for birdie but all in all, it was a good day."

And with that untypical understatement and another pot for the trophy cabinet, Poulter headed straight to the airport for his second stab at the US PGA Championship, this time being held at Rochester's Oak Hill. Such is the life of a successful Tour pro.

The win in Denmark would be Poulter's fifth victory on Tour in just 109 starts, one that sent him racing up the Volvo Order of Merit into fifth place and, thanks to the winner's cheque of €266,660, took his season's earnings over the million Euro mark. Moreover, in one sensational three-tournament spell spanning the Trophée Lancôme, the Linde German Masters and the Dunhill Links Championship – that had yielded two ties for third and a tie for 16th – he shot 11 rounds in the 60s from a possible 12.

After a ninth place finish at the Volvo Masters, Poulter settled back and reflected on a job well done. The pre-season targets had been met, there was more money in the bank than he could ever have imagined and life was sweet. Heady days indeed.

Chapter 4
Flying the Flag

@IanJamesPoulter

Show passion or your (sic) not trying simple. Don't play to take part. Play to win or don't bother playing.

The first and most keenly anticipated major of each golfing year is the Masters. Held in early April in the sumptuous surroundings of the Augusta National Golf Club, an old plant nursery brought to life by the imagination of the legendary Bobby Jones, it is an event that, for myriad reasons, really is without compare in the golfing calendar, as the world's finest players converge in Georgia to do battle for the right to wear the coveted green jacket.

Sometimes strange but always compelling, the men of the Masters run a very tight ship and they expect only the best behaviour from players and fans (although they're not "fans" as such – they are, if you will, called "patrons"). Everything is meticulously organized, from the dazzling flower beds to the dyed water hazards. There is no official tournament sponsor, nor is there any advertising on or around the golf course. And you'll never hear officially what the winner receives in terms of prize money. No, that would be far, far too vulgar.

On the face of it, you would think that the rich tradition and almost suffocating standards of the Masters might grate with a free spirit like Ian Poulter but there were immediate concerns for the Englishman ahead of his maiden appearance at Augusta in 2004. While the Masters always brought its own kind of pressure for the players, for Poulter it represented something of a medical challenge too, in that the preponderance of so much flora and fauna in the grounds played havoc with his hay fever and asthma. So, while other players might spend an hour on the practice range in preparation, Poulter would also have to repair to the medicine cabinet and apply eye drops and nasal sprays, swallow tablets and have antihistamine injections. But it didn't matter. Thanks to his two victories, six top-10 finishes and a spot in the top 10 of the European Tour's Order of Merit, he had bagged a place at Augusta and no runny nose or streaming eyes would stop him from playing.

That said, his reputation had preceded him and as the build-up to the tournament continued apace, there were rumours and reports that Augusta's autocratic chairman, William "Hootie" Johnson, had, through a third party, contacted Poulter reminding him of the standards that they maintained at the club and how fashion statements like, say, extravagantly dyed hair were frowned upon.

It was a story that Poulter was quick to refute, although his denial did lack a certain persuasion. "It's all been blown out of proportion. I don't want to make a big deal out of it," he said. "I haven't had a letter from him. And Hootie Johnson hasn't said anything to me. As far as I know he hasn't got any problem with me in any shape or form."

Instead, Poulter chose to talk about his choice of colour combinations and just how he would wear the Green Jacket, should things go to plan. "There's a rumour of a pink outfit," he hinted, "and there might be one in my bag. I wouldn't say it's all pink but

I have been known to wear pink trousers before. I haven't made up my mind – but there might be a big splash of pink on one of the first two days."

And the Green Jacket? "I'd look great in that," he smiled.

At 28, Ian Poulter was confident enough in his own skin – and with his golf game – to predict great things for his career, and the fact that he had made it to Augusta, climbing into the top 50 players in the world, was evidence that he had the talent to back it up. His was a self-belief that came naturally, although in a world as polite as professional golf, that confidence had often been construed as arrogance. Not that Poulter had any notion of changing a game-plan that had taken him so far. "I'm not going to change for anyone," he insisted. "But if you're going to be outspoken then you'd better go out there and produce some stuff to stop yourself looking a complete plonker."

But for all the trash talk, the heinous hairstyles and the fancy pants, Poulter also seemed to have an inherent sense that, while he could push the envelope in certain circumstances, there was a line that sometimes it was best not to cross. Take his appearance at Augusta. Here was a club that still refused membership and that only allowed black people to become members in 1990. Previously, the only blacks allowed at the club had been local caddies. Indeed, in 1933 Augusta's co-founder, Clifford Roberts, had said: "As long as I'm alive, all the golfers will be white and all the caddies will be black."

In theory, then, Augusta seemed to be a wholly acceptable target, an open goal if you like, for someone as vocal and outspoken as Poulter, but, instead, there was already a circumspection that verged on deference whenever he was quizzed on some of the club's more archaic policies and procedures. "The Masters is what it is," he said, tip-toeing around the issue. "It's always been pretty much the same up until now. I don't know all the ins and outs of its history. And I'm not going to say they're doing anything wrong. It's a fantastic tournament. I've always said golf can be a turn-off – all those middle-aged men in bad jumpers. I want to be a bit more of a character. But I'd never rip the Masters. I'd prefer to win it rather than just shock their members."

Besides, he knew only too well what the men of the Masters could and would do to anyone who dared to go off-message. In 1994, for instance, the CBS analyst and former PGA Tour player Gary McCord had quipped that the 17th green at Augusta was so quick it must have been "bikini-waxed", adding that there were "body bags" over the back of the hole too. Suffice to say, it wasn't the kind of language that met with approval in the committee rooms at Augusta. Soon after, McCord's accreditation for the Masters was revoked and nearly 20 years on from the incident he has yet to return to Augusta as a commentator, even though he works at every other event CBS covers.

The Masters wasn't the oldest major (the Open Championship had almost three-quarters of a century on it) nor was it always the most challenging, but what it had in spades was an atmosphere and ambience that had been as carefully cultivated as the thousands of plants and flowers that lined the golf course. There was an aura at Augusta, a unique sense that this was somewhere truly special, perhaps even heavenly. And while it had been nine years since Poulter had turned professional off a very high handicap and four years since he had joined the Tour, now he had made it to Magnolia Lane and it felt, well, right. So right, in fact, that he had even flown 12 members of his family over to Georgia to share in the experience. "Just to walk out on that first tee will be massive," he said. "I've been watching the Masters since I was a kid, and so for 20 years I've been dreaming of Augusta. It's always had a magical quality and I remember Nick Faldo's victories very clearly. Ian Woosnam's win is also vivid."

To this day, Poulter still flies friends and family out for Masters' week. In 2013, for example, he was joined not only by his mum, dad and uncle, but by Andy Day, the member of Leighton Buzzard Golf Club who once backed Poulter with £1,500 in the days when he had high hopes as a fledgling professional but little else, and Phil Abbott, his old friend from the pro shop at Leighton Buzzard.

Teeing off at 10.56am in his first round, you could get a sense of just where Poulter was in the Augusta pecking order by the players that he found himself grouped with and, while America's Jonathan Byrd and Australia's Craig Parry were undoubtedly fine players, they weren't exactly the box-office draw that Poulter had secretly hoped he might get. Still, his Masters journey was up and running and he seemed determined to wring every last ounce of enjoyment out of this unique experience.

It would be a steady if unspectacular competitive debut at Augusta and his three-over-par 75 – the same score as the world number one and three-times champion, Tiger Woods, and the game's greatest ever player, Jack Nicklaus – would see him sat in the middle of the pack at the end of a day that saw his best friend on Tour, Justin Rose, whip round Augusta in a peerless five-under-par 67 to take an early lead.

The following day, Poulter, Byrd and Parry were out first at 8am, as the dew still glistened on Augusta's pristine fairways. Armed with some added confidence (like he needed some) and some new-found local knowledge, Poulter improved his showing by two shots and his four-over par total would be enough – just – to make the cut. "It was a day of many, many, many missed chances," he said after his round. "I played fantastic but shaved the hole and horseshoed out a few times. Augusta is as tough as I thought it would be. Fantastic! What a place to come and play golf."

It was job done. Poulter had made the cut while the likes of his two playing partners, the reigning champion from Canada, Mike Weir, and former great champions like Jack Nicklaus, Nick Faldo, Ian Woosnam and Tom Watson all fell by the wayside. It was a fine achievement and although the weekend failed to see him mount any kind of sustained assault on the leaderboard, his final placing of a tie for 31st was a satisfactory end to his maiden Masters.

But it would be a Masters to remember for other reasons. While Phil Mickelson would finally shed the tag of being the best player never to win a major, bagging one of the big four after 42 attempts, it would also mark the final playing appearance at the Masters – his 50th in a row – of the four-time winner and living legend Arnold Palmer. And so what if Poulter had finished 16 shots behind Mickelson, he had made it to Augusta and, more than that, he had held his own in some exalted company.

Ticking the Masters off his to-do list was just one of the things Poulter had earmarked for 2004. In an interview with the *Guardian* ahead of the event, he had also mapped out his plans for the rest of the year, picking out one particular competition he had always been determined to get involved in. "I don't have any doubts about making the Ryder Cup team. It's not an issue," he insisted. "I'm gonna make the team and I've got the dream scenario: Tiger and me head-to-head on the Sunday. We're in the final match and everything comes down to our result, which gets decided on the 18th hole.

Chapter 4

That would be the utmost pressure. I've never been in anything that intense, but I'd love to put myself through it and come out on top."

But first he would have to make Bernhard Langer's team and that would require form above and beyond the kind he was showing in the spring of 2004. After the Masters, Poulter had struggled to a tie for 61st at the MCI Heritage the following week at Harbour Town in South Carolina, before returning home to the European Tour for a string of events across the continent. At the Italian Open, the tournament he had won back in 2000, he had finished in a creditable tie for sixth but, once again, all the talk had not been about his golf. During his first-round 68, Poulter had become irritated by a mobile phone going off in the galleries and, rather than get the marshals to investigate, had taken matters into his own hands and simply snatched the offending device from the spectator and thrown it straight in the bin. It was a zero tolerance approach that seemed to work for Poulter, but not, perhaps, for the fan's phone.

After a tie for 20th at the British Masters at the Forest of Arden the following week, Poulter had travelled over to Germany for the Deutsche-Bank SAP Open TPC of Europe still in search of the little spark that might ignite his season. But having completed his second round he had received news that back home in England his partner Katie was going into labour with the couple's second child. Withdrawing immediately from the tournament, he hot-footed it to the airport, but it was no good: Luke Poulter, the boy he had wanted, would come into the world without his daddy there to welcome him.

Such were the perils of being a professional golfer. Here, after all, is a vocation that's hardly conducive to a good marriage or family life, a job where being away from home for weeks on end and living out

58

of a suitcase are as much part of the game as putting the ball in the hole. Missing Luke's birth, then, must have convinced Poulter that he needed to lay down some roots on a more permanent basis and, given the way his career was progressing and the many ambitions he still harboured as a player that, inevitably, meant moving Katie and the kids full-time to the United States.

That's not to say life was one endless slog around anonymous hotels and one clubhouse after another, far from it, and Poulter's reputation as one of the merry-makers of the Tour and a player who occasionally cocked a snook at some of the more antiquated elements of the game was one that was now beginning to precede him. For the most part, Poulter's antics – if they could really be labelled as such – were always, at the very least, entertaining and while he wasn't (and never will be) flavour of the month with the game's blazer brigade or a certain section of golf fans, his behaviour never really crossed the line. Besides, there was no knowing what would cause upset among some people in the game.

Take the debacle that surrounded his now infamous Union Jack trousers at that year's Open Championship at Royal Troon in Scotland. Loud, proud and designed by his friend and Savile Row tailor, William Hunt, the trousers would come to dominate the headlines but were, more than anything, an observation on the super-serious world of professional golf rather than any comment on Poulter's taste in clothes. He had originally planned to unveil the trousers at the US Open at Shinnecock Hills, but had decided to hold them back for his home Open instead. Now, he had emerged on the first tee with the kind of legwear that could have sparked an international incident. Traditionalists were horrified, children startled and reporters excited. And yet it was only a pair of trousers.

With a Kangol-style TaylorMade beret on his head completing the look, some said Poulter had taken to the course looking every inch the golf guerrilla, a Che Guevara with a gap wedge, if you like. Others said he looked like the seventies sitcom star Frank Spencer.

Still, if Poulter's aim was to garner some column inches then it was mission accomplished. The following day, the UK's biggest-selling tabloid, the *Sun*, splashed him right across the front page, while other newspapers carried reports about how the Royal & Ancient had borne the brunt of golf fans' ire. "Our switchboard has received a lot of complaints today about Ian's trousers," confirmed the R&A's chief executive Peter Dawson. "There is no clause in the rules which says anything about Union Jack trousers and we shall not be asking Ian to change them. Ian is known for trying to be different with his appearance and all you can do is hope players adhere to the dress code on the European Tour. I wonder what he has in store for tomorrow?"

There were a couple of issues arising from what the tabloids had thankfully refrained from calling "Trouser-Gate". The first was that the R&A's bible, *The Rules Of Golf*, did not contain anything that might have prevented Poulter from wearing what was, in effect, a national flag wrapped around his legs. It would have been interesting what he, and the R&A for that matter, would have done had the Open been held at Royal Portrush or Royal County Down in Northern Ireland, for example.

The second issue, meanwhile, was that here was a sport with a history of dreadful crimes against fashion, not to mention elitism and sexism, that had gone largely unnoticed for years, a fact Poulter was only too keen to point out when quizzed about his trousers later. Royal Troon Golf Club operated a strict "no female members" policy even in the twenty-first century, but no one had seen fit to take the R&A to task about that, only, it seemed, the fact that Poulter's new trousers were a little on the bright side. "What do I say to the fact that some people have complained? They are a pair of trousers, that's what I say," he said, quite reasonably. "They are a normal pair of trousers, it is just that they are pretty colourful. I am always trying to be different and do something different. I don't like the way most people dress on the golf course, I think it is pretty bland. Wearing khaki or black trousers is boring stuff and although what I wear isn't everyone's cup of tea it is the way I am."

If Peter Dawson appeared relaxed about just what Poulter had planned for his wardrobe for the rest of the most important week in the R&A's calendar, then there must have been a part of him that wondered just how far the player was prepared to take his sartorial statements at Royal Troon.

He needn't have worried. For the next three days, Poulter reined it, although his look was anything but conventional. Retro perhaps, but not conventional. Yes, with a doff of the cap – literally – to the late Payne Stewart, Friday's outfit saw him teaming black top and beret with white plus-fours and black-and-white diamond socks, Saturday was a dark blue outfit with plus-fours, pink socks and beret, no less, while Sunday's crowd-pleasing ensemble introduced a Caledonian theme, as he ended his Open challenge with tartan plus-fours, white shirt and black beret.

After the rather unnecessary furore surrounding the Union Jack trousers at the Open Championship, Poulter had turned his attentions to what he might wear at the final major of the year, the PGA Championship at the Pete Dye masterpiece, Whistling Straits in Kohler, Wisconsin. There he would turn up in a lurid pair of stars and stripes trousers, with the stripes down the right leg and the stars all the way down the left. It was a good bit of PR on Poulter's part and a great way to ingratiate himself with a country that would soon become his home, but once was funny and twice was pushing it. Besides, where would it end? Would there be a hammer and sickle when he next played the Russian Open? Or maybe a fire-breathing dragon on his posterior for a trip to Celtic Manor?

In time, of course, Poulter's predilection for revealing new trousers, especially at major championships, would not just become commonplace – and expected – but actually quite tiresome, especially as it distracted from just how good a golfer he had become. At the following year's Open Championship at St Andrews, for example, he even threw the choice of his trousers open to the readers of the BBC Sport's website, inviting designs as part of a "Design Poulter's Pants" competition to have his trousers made for the first round of the tournament.

Two thousand responses would pour in, with the winning entry coming from 35-year-old Gavin Adams, from Oxfordshire. The resulting trousers, meanwhile, were arguably even more hideous than anything Poulter had worn previously, featuring an enormous Claret Jug (complete with plinth) running down the bottom half of one leg and a roll call of all of the previous Open Championship winners on the back of the other. "Last year's Union Jack trousers were outrageous," explained Poulter as he met with the competition winner, "but these trousers have got enough statement in them."

Quite what that statement was, of course, was open to debate and actually dependant on one's own extremely subjective stance on what passed for fashion, but when Poulter finally revealed the trousers at the Home of Golf, they became another hot topic for discussion.

Perhaps the funniest critique, however, would come from the three-time winner Seve Ballesteros. Working in the commentary box, when the Spanish legend saw Poulter breeze past, he remarked that the trousers might be "the closest he would ever get to" the Claret Jug.

As it transpired, Poulter would go on to finish in a tie for 11th place at St Andrews. It would be his best ever result at the Open Championship and eclipsed the tie for 25th that he and his flag-pants would registered in 2004. The finish at Royal Troon would, however, still give him some invaluable points in his quest to qualify for Europe's Ryder Cup team and as Poulter went into the final qualifying event for the matches at Oakland Hills, the BMW International at Munich's Eichenried Golf Club, he knew precisely what he had to do to qualify for Bernhard Langer's team: a finish of 45th or better would be sufficient to see him make his first appearance in the event that had captivated him since he was a child.

Though he started with a one-over-par 73, his next two rounds of 66 and 69 saw Poulter head into the final, all-important round in a tie for 18th and just seven shots off the leaders, Spain's Miguel Angel Jimenez and France's Thomas Levet. More importantly, though, he was in prime position for Ryder Cup qualification.

But there was disaster waiting for him at the 10th. Though his round was progressing nicely and his Ryder Cup place seemed assured, Poulter suddenly conspired to hit not one but two balls into the water at the par-four hole and the resulting quadruple bogey sent him plummeting down the leaderboard and into 45th place, the very last position he could finish if he was to prevent the Swede Freddie Jacobson from stealing his Ryder Cup place.

Meanwhile, back at the offices of *Golf Punk* magazine there was blind panic. Having decided to feature Poulter on the cover of their special Ryder Cup issue with a huge coverline that screamed how Europe were going to win the contest, the editorial team were now praying that Poulter could somehow save them from what appeared to be publishing suicide. "We were already at the printers awaiting our slot wondering what on earth we had done," explained editor-in-chief Tim Southwell. "There we were, looking like we were going to have our Ryder Cup issue with a player on the cover that, in all likelihood, wasn't even going to be there. It didn't look good."

Of course, it would have been entirely understandable if Poulter had crumbled given the pressure of the situation unfolding before him, but the manner of his response was nothing short of phenomenal and revealed a player with guts, determination and guile. At the very next hole, he made an eagle three and then closed with birdies at the 15th and 16th before making another eagle three at the last. As his ball disappeared from view, Poulter's relief was tangible as he threw his black visor in the air and was patted heartily on the back by his friend and playing partner, Darren Clarke.

By picking up a remarkable six shots in his last eight holes, Poulter's two-under par round had given him a share of 25th place and he had not only secured his Ryder Cup place, he had shown precisely the kind of spirit that would be needed in spades at Oakland Hills, come the showdown in mid-September.

On the scorecard it may have said "70", but that round would have felt like a 59 and Poulter, quite understandably, was pumped. "The guys kept saying, come on, make some birdies. After that quadruple bogey, I went into overdrive," he said after his round. "I played some unbelievable golf."

Back at *Golf Punk* magazine, meanwhile, the nervousness had also given way to relief and celebration. "When he made that quadruple bogey at the 10th we thought we'd blown it too," added Southwell. "But then he goes and plays the last eight holes in six-under par, making two eagles, and suddenly we're all left wondering what the problem was. We should never have doubted him really."

For the first time since 1981, Europe would field a Ryder Cup team without a single major winner in it and where once a Ballesteros or a Faldo, a Lyle or a Woosnam would have shouldered the burden of responsibility, now the duty fell to experienced veterans like Darren Clarke, Lee Westwood, Padraig Harrington and the captain's pick, Colin Montgomerie, who would now be playing in his seventh consecutive Ryder Cup.

Leading them into battle at the course once described by Ben Hogan as a "monster" would be Germany's double-Masters champion and Ryder Cup stalwart, Bernhard Langer. Meticulous and methodical, Langer's approach to the captaincy saw him involved in every facet of the job; he even chose the wine for the team meals and the post-meal cigars. "Langer was probably the best of our captains in every aspect," argued the PGA's then chief executive Sandy Jones. "He was totally professional. There was nothing left to chance. Everything was perfect in that Germanic sort of way."

Indeed, Langer was so thorough that he also researched the psychological impact of the colours that his team should wear, making notes as to which combinations made the players feel confident and comfortable. The only question was whether Ian Poulter, a player who wouldn't wear just any old togs, would find the cut and the style of the European team uniforms to his liking. "I'm happy to wear any uniform this week. No matter what it is," he insisted. "Since I followed it in '93, I just wanted to wear it with the crest. And whether it be funky pullovers or whether it be nicely-tailored trousers, I really don't mind."

Langer's methodology was designed to take what was, in effect, a disparate and nebulous assembly of men and help mould them into something that was greater than its individual parts. During their practice rounds, he would walk with his players, telling them how to approach a hole or play a particular shot and it was a mark of the esteem in which he was held among the team that he felt he could tell these millionaires how to play the game without finding a four-iron wrapped around his neck.

But then Langer was just applying the same kind of attention to detail to his captaincy as he had experienced when playing at the Ryder Cup. Famously, when he was partnering Colin Montgomerie at the "War On The Shore" Ryder Cup at Kiawah Island in 1991, he had asked the Scot to pace out the yardage from a sprinkler head to the front of the putting surface. Dutifully, the young debutant went off and paced it out for his senior partner before returning. "Nineteen paces," he said, keenly.

"Was that from the front or the back of the sprinkler?" replied Langer.

Langer's opposite number, meanwhile, was the 1983 PGA champion and four-time Ryder Cup player Hal Sutton. As usual, the American skipper had at his disposal an array of major winners and household names, but his central concern was the relationship between the greatest player of his generation, Tiger Woods, and the world number two, Phil Mickelson. For years, rumours of a marked antipathy between the two had persisted and in a bid to get them working together and back on track, Sutton had decided to send them out in the first morning's foursomes.

Along with David Howell, Poulter would sit out the first day's
play, but if he had ever needed confirmation of just how intense
playing in the Ryder Cup could be, it came when he took his place
on the sidelines to watch Woods and Mickelson, two players with
63 PGA tour titles between them, tee off on that opening day. "I tell
you, when I stood there and saw Tiger hit it 50 yards right of the
fairway and then Mickelson hit it 50 yards left, it didn't matter where
I hit," he laughed. "You had the number one and number two in the
world and they couldn't even get it to within 50 yards of the fairway.
That settled me down a treat. I was there, I saw them – yhey were
shaking. Mind you, had they striped it down the middle, it might
have been a different story."

Europe would end that first day with a commanding 6½–1½
lead – the biggest first day lead in the history of the Ryder Cup.
All of Langer's preparation and his decisions had been vindicated,
even leaving Poulter on the sidelines. But having sat out a day
when the Europeans had silenced what had been a raucous crowd,
Poulter would make his Ryder Cup debut in Saturday morning's
fourballs. Paired with the Ulsterman Darren Clarke, the steadiest
of Ryder Cup hands, he would find himself up against another
debutant, Chris Riley, and the man he had laughed at the previous
day and a man with eight major titles under his belt, Tiger Woods.
Hailing from California, Riley had known Tiger from their time
in junior golf when they had often teamed up to play together. On
the Friday evening, when Sutton had told the 30-year-old former
Walker Cup player that he was now going to be playing with
Woods, Riley had, by his own admission, "Free-wheeled" out of the
United States team room, so delighted was he to be playing with
the world's best golfer again.

It would be a baptism of fire for Poulter. Having gone one down at the opening hole, the European duo were powerless to prevent Woods and Riley powering into an even bigger lead and their 4&3 victory was as comprehensive as it suggested. Suddenly, Poulter knew exactly what the Ryder Cup was all about – and it wasn't giggling at Woods and Mickelson firing it sideways off the first tee.

Woods and Riley's win would set up a 2½–1½ session win for the home side and already the sense that the United States were set to mount one of their trademark comebacks was hard to ignore. For once, though, US hope would be fleeting. Come the afternoon, Langer had reinvigorated his troops and a 3–1 session win in the foursomes, the highlight of which was Padraig Harrington and Paul McGinley's brutal 4&3 destruction of Davis Love III and Woods, helped Europe into an 11–5 lead going into the Sunday singles. It was the biggest ever lead in Ryder Cup history and one that Europe were not going to surrender.

Come the singles and Poulter's "dream scenario" of him going head-to-head with Tiger would fail to materialize – but then that was probably a good thing as Woods looked imperious in grinding down Paul Casey 3&2. Instead, Poulter would have to content himself with a singles match against the other half of the duo that had beaten him and Darren Clarke so emphatically on Saturday: Chris Riley.

Typically, the US has tended to reserve its strongest Ryder Cup performances for the Sunday singles matches but at Oakland Hills there seemed to be nothing left in the tank and if Woods' dominant showing at the top end of the line-up had been designed to kick-start another resurgence it had largely fallen flat. Apart from one-sided wins for Jim Furyk over David Howell and Chad Campbell over Luke Donald and Chris DiMarco's last-hole victory over Miguel

Angel Jimenez, there would be no other US wins on Sunday, and when Lee Westwood pipped Kenny Perry at the 18th, Europe was on the brink of another famous victory.

With attention turning to the remaining games left out on the golf course, the only question was who would be the hero of the hour for Europe? For once, Colin Montgomerie, so long the beating heart of the European team, hadn't been thrust forward to lead the singles. Instead, Bernhard Langer opted to put the Scot out in the middle order as if he knew, by virtue of his meticulous planning, that the match would come down to his old Ryder Cup playing partner.

Requiring a par at the 18th to record a one-hole win over David Toms (and maintain his record of never having lost in Ryder Cup singles), Montgomerie stood over a four-foot par putt to win his game and the Ryder Cup. When the putt dropped, inevitably, he simply dropped his putter on the green and walked over to his team-mates to bask in the glory of a memorable moment. Europe had won a famous victory and Montgomerie had made the winning putt.

Or had he? Back at the 15th hole, Poulter had just holed a birdie putt in his game against Chris Riley to go three up with three to play, meaning that he was guaranteed at least half a point. Crucially, it was, as TV and radio reports showed, moments before Montgomerie holed his final putt. BBC Radio 5 Live's golf correspondent Iain Carter explained later: "My editor said Poulter was three up seconds before Monty hit his putt," he recalled. "Then Colin's putt went in – you can imagine the situation. To have overruled his achievement would have been like trying to deny Alan Shearer a goal that went in off a defender."

It was an intriguing situation and the only issue, it seemed, was that as Poulter was now dormie in his match (i.e. he couldn't lose) the game had not officially ended and there was still the possibility, remote though it may have been, that something untoward could have happened and Poulter could have been disqualified and therefore lost his match. When I interviewed Poulter in 2008, he was still unsure as to who had actually hit the winning putt in the record-breaking victory at Oakland Hills. "Did I hole the winning putt? Well, yes and no," he said. "I'd holed a putt to secure a half point against Chris Riley but my game wasn't actually finished so there's two ways of looking at it. But you know, it doesn't really matter who holes the winning putt. It's a team event. It's not about individuals."

Irrespective of the true identity of the hero of the hour, Poulter's first point in the Ryder Cup had been won and any disappointment he may have felt from missing out on the first day and then losing heavily in his only other match in Saturday's morning fourballs soon evaporated. Of course, in the grand scheme of things, it wouldn't have mattered a jot if Poulter had not managed to beat Riley as a comprehensive European victory had all but been confirmed by the end of play on Saturday, but for Poulter, pointless up until that moment, it had meant everything, as he explained in the aftermath of victory. "Obviously I was disappointed with losing a point yesterday. [But] I focused well this morning and the guys said don't look at the leaderboards. I did want to look – I always look at them all my life. I had a quick glimpse and it was a sea of red, not what I wanted to see. And I guess that made me focus a little bit harder. I did do that. I really wanted to put a point on the board for the team, I just wanted to make up for losing a point yesterday. And that was really pleasing for me to do that for the team."

As the celebrations began and Thomas Levet attempted to drown himself in champagne, Poulter was coming to terms with his first taste of the Ryder Cup experience. More importantly, he was savouring the rare and incomparable taste of a Ryder Cup victory on American soil. After the presentation of the trophy, he decided that it was high time he finally hogged some of the limelight and began aeroplaning round the 18th green with a European flag tucked into his pocket and a Union Jack draped around his neck as a makeshift cravat. Even when the team made its flight home to Heathrow, Poulter still seemed reluctant to relinquish the trophy, placing it in the cot alongside his new son Luke as he slept, oblivious to the fact he was wrapped in a signed Ryder Cup flag from Oakland Hills.

But if Poulter needed more concrete proof of the significance of the European team's victory in America it came a month after that heady day at Oakland Hills. Back in the United Kingdom, he had made another pilgrimage to Highbury to watch Arsenal play Aston Villa where, before the game kicked off, he was invited on to the pitch to parade the Ryder Cup in front of the crowd. And as if to say thanks, Arsenal had returned the favour, winning the game 3–1. Playing Tiger and Phil – and winning – was one thing but walking out in front of the Clock End with the Ryder Cup in his hands? That would take some beating.

Even in the strange and sometimes surreal world of Ian Poulter, 2004 had been more than a little bonkers. Before the year was out, he would discover that his celebrity, as a Ryder Cup hero, had exploded beyond anything he could have reasonably anticipated. Soon, he would have his concreted handprint made and displayed in the new flagship adidas store on London's Oxford Street and he would stride down the catwalk dressed only in a silk dressing gown at a fashion event at Wentworth. He would team up with Hollywood A-lister Dennis Hopper at the Dunhill Links Championship, he would play golf with the McLaren Formula One driver Juan-Pablo Montoya and he would also perform on stage with the Boyzone star Ronan Keating during the Nelson Mandela Invitational at the Arabella Country Estate. He would even meet Mr Mandela himself and, today, he has a signed painting of the great man hanging above his fireplace. Poulter that is, not Mandela.

But if it seemed that Poulter might be taking his eye off the golf ball as the demands on his time away from the course escalated, it couldn't have been further from the truth. For many golfers and, indeed, athletes more generally, the impact of a big win or some sudden and stunning success often results in an almost instant impact on their form. For Poulter, however, it represented a new opportunity, a chance to build on something quite special and reinforce his claim to be one of the world's best golfers.

At the season-ending Volvo Masters at Europe's own Augusta, Valderrama, in Sotogrande, Spain, Poulter brought the curtain down on a solid year in spectacular style when, just five weeks after the heroics in Michigan, he defeated his Ryder Cup team-mate Sergio Garcia in a sudden-death play-off to win the title and what would be the biggest cheque of his career (€625,000). The win not only propelled him to ninth on the final European Tour Order of Merit, with €1,533,158, but also gave him a five-year exemption to the Tour. Moreover, he could now have automatic entry in all four majors in 2005, as well as the lucrative World Golf Championship events too.

The win also opened up the possibility of Poulter playing on a more regular basis on the PGA Tour. It was something that he was clearly keen to exploit. "I've got an opportunity to go out there and play. I think the European Tour will always be my home. I've loved my golf over here. I'm a very happy player here. I will always play my quota, if not more than my quota of events. But, you know, I do think that I do have to play a few events in America which do hold a few more world ranking points than maybe a few of the ones in Europe. That's key to me moving higher in the world rankings, and that's what it's all about, being able to give yourself the opportunity to get into the Top 20, the Top 10 and hopefully higher."

It was a view reinforced by Poulter's manager, Paul Dunkley. "If you look at the world ranking points that are available between the two tours, there's almost twice as many on offer in America," said Dunkley. "There are 30–50 people who consider themselves global golfers and want to be in the top 20 in the world, but to do that you have to play in the US because the world ranking points are much greater. It becomes almost self-fulfilling – the more you play, the more world ranking points are available."

When Poulter's final short par putt dropped at the 18th and he began celebrating, on rushed his daughter Aimee-Leigh to join in, rocking her dad back on his haunches and giving the sponsors the kind of family, feel-good image they would be more than happy to see splashed across the sports media the following day. It was great for the Poulter brand too. "It was unbelievable to come here this week and win," he reflected. "I felt I shouldn't be satisfied with the way my year had panned out. I had played OK but not managed to finish anything off. This is a sweet end to the year and to cap it all with a win in the Volvo Masters Andalucia turned an average year into quite a nice one."

Which begged the question: if this was just an "average year" for Poulter, what exactly would constitute a good one?

As it transpired, though, 2004 would end up being the kind of campaign that Poulter would have gladly swapped for 2005, given the overwhelmingly disappointing manner in which it developed. Of course, it's as inevitable as a bland Tiger Woods press conference, that golfers will suffer a loss of form from time to time. The issue is how you deal with it and overcome it.

For Poulter, already accustomed to the high life of being a Tour winner in each season he had played, 2005 represented the most frustrating of his professional career to date and it seemed that he couldn't buy a top-10 finish yet alone another title.

His performance in the majors was typical of the way the year would unravel. There was a tie for 33rd at the Masters, a tie for 57th at the US Open and a tie for 47th at the US PGA. The only chink of light among the unremitting gloom was a tie for 11th at the Open Championship – his best-ever finish in the event – but even then it wasn't as if he was challenging the leaders, just picking up places when the tournament was already out of his reach.

At times, it also seemed as though fate was conspiring to keep him down, as if all the crazy haircuts and snappy strides had suddenly appeared on the golf gods' radar, incurring their wrath. You could tell that his mediocre form may well have been getting to him too, as now little things were suddenly big issues. When Poulter went into the US Open in mid-June, for example, he did so on the back of a worryingly poor recent track record on the PGA Tour. In his previous four events, he had missed three out of four cuts, with only a tie for 30th at Jack Nicklaus' Memorial tournament at Muirfield Village in Ohio, punctuating a miserable run.

Having made his US Open debut at Shinnecock Hills 12 months earlier, Poulter had returned to the tournament, this time being held at the fearsome and revered Pinehurst No.2 in North Carolina, intent on at least making the cut this time around. It wasn't going to be easy. Of all the four majors, the US Open was always the one that returned the highest totals, chiefly because the organizers, the United States Golf Association (USGA) set their host courses in such a way that a low score is almost impossible and, it's often thought, to bring the world's best players down a peg or two in the process. With tight, narrow fairways and the kind of penal rough in which you could quite easily lose small children, the USGA's US Open golf courses were about as user-friendly as a chainsaw and often more dangerous.

During his opening round (and having started at the 10th hole) Poulter had reached the 18th when his tap-in for par almost popped out of the hole. On closer inspection, he looked down to find that the rim of the hole hadn't been buried deeply enough in the ground, the result being that his ball had hit the protruding rim and almost refused to drop.

But at the very next hole, the same thing happened again and this time, his ball rebounded back off the rim and stayed out of the cup. Summoning over a tournament official, Poulter pointed out the defective cup, but to his amazement, the official ruled that the holes were perfect for play. Before they moved on to the second, Poulter made a point of forcing the cup down with the flag, just so others didn't have to suffer the same fate.

But he wasn't happy. "I'm choosing my words very, very, very, very politely at the minute," he fumed. "The rough's three inches thick out there. It's difficult to hit the fairways. The greens are drying out. There are enough things to think about without wondering whether the hole's actually been pushed down an inch or not, especially when you hit the perfect putt and it comes back at you. It's a mistake which shouldn't happen."

It was an angle and an opening gambit that Poulter would often use in post-round interviews when he wanted to criticize someone or something, but needed a way of reminding himself not to say what he really wanted to. In the future, of course, he would have another vehicle, Twitter, to get his point across, but for now, he had to make do with the press conference. "There's nothing I can do," he added. "They (tournament officials) feel like the hole was an inch down. I'm telling you it wasn't. I think the hole on 18 is borderline being an inch pushed down and the one on one is not down an inch."

Most golfers, whether first-timers or battle-weary veterans, rarely opt to make public their concerns, let alone openly criticize the golf course at a major championship. It's just not the done thing. For someone like Poulter to come out, in just his second appearance and at a tournament as esteemed and respected as the US Open, and vent his spleen was surprising on one hand and quite welcome on the other. But it still didn't mask what was another dire day at the office and Poulter's first-round 77 left him way down the leaderboard at 113th and in grave danger of missing the cut once more. Commendably, he would rally in his second round, posting a one-under par round of 69 to make the cut mark by two strokes.

But Poulter's point about matters being hard enough at the US Open without any extra obstacles being introduced was certainly borne out by the scores posted in the rest of the competition. While Ian's next two rounds of 74 and 76 saw him end with what, on the face of it, looked like a staggeringly high total of 16-over par, in the warped world of the US Open it really wasn't that bad, especially as the last placed player that made the cut, America's Jerry Kelly, came in at 25-over and the winner, New Zealand's Michael Campbell, took the title with an even-par total of 280.

Of course, the US Open was the tournament that the USGA were perhaps the most protective of and the idea that any of their champion golfers should ever shoot anything under-par seemed to be anathema to them. In 2011, for instance, Rory McIlroy, the prodigiously talented young man from Northern Ireland, hadn't just won the US Open at Congressional Country Club in Maryland, he had decimated the field, winning by eight shots and, much to the USGA's chagrin, dismantled the actual course too, scoring four rounds in the 60s and setting 11 US Open records along the way, including the lowest winning total – 16-under par – in the long and illustrious history of the event. The following year, however, it was business as usual at the US Open as the USGA, doubtless irked by McIlroy's impudence, set up the Lake Course at San Francisco's Olympic Club with real spite, and Webb Simpson's winning score of +1 was a sure sign the organizers were not prepared to be embarrassed for a second successive year.

While his form was a major concern – it had to be – it wasn't for lack of trying. Indeed, it is one of Poulter's many strengths that irrespective of the mad world that he seems to inhabit from time to time, his application and work ethic has always been a key part of his success. It's a drive and a determination that has come to typify his career and goes a long way to explain his rise from golf shop assistant to millionaire sportsman. Observers may see the conspicuous displays of wealth – the flashy clothes, the sports cars, the houses here, there and everywhere – but his isn't a story of inherited wealth or good fortune on a grand scale. Put simply, you need to put the hours in and Poulter, whatever you may think of him, has certainly done that.

In fact, it's a work ethic that has, at times, got him into trouble, most notably at the Seve Trophy in 2005, where his determination to right some wrongs in his game ended up backfiring spectacularly. First played in 2000, the Seve Trophy was the European Tour's home-made version of the Ryder Cup, named after and played in honour of the Tour's leading light, Seve Ballesteros, and contested by teams from Great Britain and Ireland and from Continental Europe. In 2005, for the match at Teesside's Wynyard Golf Club, the British team would be captained by the Ryder Cup stalwart and man with one eye on the Ryder Cup captaincy itself, Colin Montgomerie.

Having qualified for the 10-man team by virtue of his performances on the European Tour and not through his world ranking (which was heading south at a rate of knots), Poulter's place saw him team up with a host of other Ryder Cup players, including Padraig Harrington, Paul McGinley, Paul Casey and David Howell. But for the first day's fourballs he had been paired with the European Tour's Rookie of the Year in 2002 and the former World Boys champion, Nick Dougherty.

Drawn against the Swedish duo of Thomas Bjorn and Henrik Stenson for the opening day's fourballs, the pair had lost by two holes and, irritated by the state of his game, Poulter had headed straight off to the practice range to work on a few issues. But with GB&I losing 3–1 in the first day's fourballs and with just one game left out on the course, Montgomerie's team had gathered around the 18th green to see how Padraig Harrington and Paul McGinley would fare in their tight match against the French pair Thomas Levet and Jean-François Remesy. That is to say, all of Montgomerie's team except Ian Poulter, an absence that had infuriated the GB&I skipper, who promptly marched over to the range to get some answers.

Tempers flared and words were exchanged with the *Sun* even reporting that Poulter had told Montgomerie to "f*** off". Later, Montgomerie explained why he had chosen to confront Poulter. "He was the only man who was not with his team," he said. "That's fine, but there are times to work on your game and we all felt that was not the appropriate time."

Poulter, meanwhile, was unusually contrite. "Nobody is going to be happy, are they?" he said. "Monty came over and said Harrington wasn't overly happy that I was hitting balls while they were playing, even though I had stopped in between all of their putts. That's fine. Absolutely fine. No problems whatsoever. I felt I needed to hit a few golf balls. Maybe I should have done it after everyone had finished. So on my side it might have been a bit of a mistake. I should have been around the 18th green watching everyone finish."

Fortunately, no lasting damage had been done to team morale and come the end of the singles on Sunday, Montgomerie's men would emerge as comfortable winners over José-Maria Olazábal's European side, taking the trophy by 16½ points to 11½. And though Montgomerie would announce publicly that any issues between the pair had been resolved and resolved instantly, as did Poulter ("Lesson learned, and that is it," he shrugged), the incident would prove to be the first in a sporting soap opera that would entertain golf fans for years to come.

Of course, there have been many rivalries in professional golf but, generally speaking, they tend to be head-to-heads that don't go much beyond the golf course. In most respects, they are professional rather than personal; Sarazen and Hagen, Nicklaus and Palmer, Snead versus Hogan – these were players who gave their all on the golf course, contesting tournaments with a rare and ferocious determination.

A good or, better still, a bad rivalry is a sports editor's dream. That's why the media today are so desperate for the resurgent Tiger Woods to finally start going toe-to-toe with the young pretender to his throne, Rory McIlory, simply because there are no genuinely or at least potentially explosive rivalries in the higher echelons of the modern game. As yet, though, that particular face-off hasn't really materialized, which means the readers, viewers and golf fans the world over will just have to wait until the next instalment of Poulter versus Montgomerie comes along, which, if recent history tells us anything, it almost certainly will.

Incidents like the episode at the Seve Trophy seemed to be the only things that were getting Poulter noticed in 2005. Certainly, it wasn't his golf. It didn't matter whether it was on the European Tour or the PGA Tour, the heady days of 2004 seemed further away than ever. Cuts were being missed with regularity, especially in the United States, and top-10 finishes were conspicuous by their absence.

But if things weren't exactly going Poulter's way on the golf course – and it wasn't through lack of application – then his life off the course couldn't have been much better. There was a new £1.5 million house for the family, situated in the countryside just outside Woburn, that boasted five bedrooms, a couple of acres and its own 165-yard practice range, where Poulter could work on his wedges. As Woburn Golf Club's Touring professional it made sense to have a base near the club and, besides, it was a nice part of the world too, familiar and friendly.

There were also innumerable opportunities presenting themselves for Poulter to indulge his passion for sport, some of which were just too good to pass up. He met England's football superstar David Beckham. And he would be invited onto one of his favourite television shows, Sky's Saturday morning football magazine programme, *Soccer AM*, for the first of what would be many appearances on the show. Given his love and knowledge of football and Arsenal FC, Poulter would be an ideal guest on the show and where some "celebrities" often turned up professing love for a particular club before invariably admitting that they never found the time to go and see them play, Poulter was wonderfully different. "Ian Poulter is always a pleasure to have on a TV show as he's a genuinely top bloke," says the programme's creator and former presenter Tim Lovejoy. "He's charismatic and a great laugh. Spending time with him is an experience, he's so positive with this amazing drive to win. His Ryder Cup record speaks volumes for his desire to succeed and how he motivates those around him. He's going to be one of the great Ryder Cup captains one day... I'd also let him in the Arsenal dressing room if I was Arsène Wenger."

The beauty of Poulter's burgeoning fame and, for that matter, his fortune, was that it now afforded him the kind of experiences on and off the golf course that any normal sports fan would give one or more limbs for. Take the Alfred Dunhill Links Championships in September, for instance. Here was an annual tournament (and one of the most lucrative on the European Tour) that saw Tour professionals paired with celebrity players for rounds around Carnoustie, Kingsbarns and St Andrews. In 2005, Poulter had been paired with the Hollywood actor Dennis Hopper in the event and the two immediately hit it off. The *Apolcalypse Now* and *Easy Rider* star had only taken up golf in his 50s when he had been introduced to the game by the country singer Willie Nelson as a way of keeping him out of bars and out of trouble. Now, he was teeing it up at the Home of Golf with a slightly star-struck Poulter standing by, watching in awe.

For that week in Scotland, the courses were awash with the great and not so good celebrity golfers. From Hugh Grant to Andy Garcia, Michael Douglas to Bill Murray, here was a tournament that not only promised a bumper pay day but also a few choice photo opportunities to be framed and hung in the study or downstairs loo. For Poulter, though, there was a chance of the kind of experience that money just can't buy. On the Tuesday before the tournament began, he decided to make a trip to Holland to see Arsenal play their Champions League tie against Ajax. But this being Poulter, there was no chance we would take a scheduled flight over to Amsterdam. No, this required a private plane and, more than that, it required a suitably impressive guest to take along for the ride. Step forward one of the celebrity golfers from that competition, none other than the Holland and Ajax legend, Johan Cruyff.

Poulter would return to Scotland the happier of the two as his team pinched a 2–1 victory. Cruyff, meanwhile, was less than impressed with what he saw, declaring it to be a "very poor game".

But Poulter's own result in Scotland would not be nearly as satisfying, however, as a tie for 52nd merely continued a sorry run that hadn't seen him bag a top-10 finish since the Scottish Open at Loch Lomond in July and take only two top 10s in the whole of the year. Even a tie for 10th in defence of his Volvo Masters title did little to offer any hope for the year ahead. It was time to make some decisions. Time to knuckle down.

Chapter 5
Fine Times

@RobbieSavage8

@IanJamesPoulter stop making an arse of yourself with your clothes pal they are ridiculous less is more!

@IanJamesPoulter

@RobbieSavage8 @therealdjspoony im quite happy knowing i own a business that is making money, if u owned 1 it would be called chavtastic

An excerpt from the infamous Twitter wars between Ian Poulter and former professional footballer Robbie Savage, October 2010

As the 2005 season had seen Poulter trying to establish himself on the PGA Tour, the mixed bag of results he had experienced across the pond, coupled with endless schleps across the Atlantic had also impacted on his form back home. While he had climbed to 15th on the European Tour money list – and had done so by playing in eight fewer events than in 2004 – his returns had dipped under £1 million for the first time since 2002 and, more worryingly, his stroke average per round had climbed from 70.72 to 71.33.

It was a similar story in his PGA Tour statistics, where his stroke average was broadly the same as in Europe (71.26) but where such a record left him nearly three shots a round worse off than Tiger Woods at the very top of the table. It was bad enough playing against someone as dominant as Woods, a golfer who was winning almost a third of the events that he entered, compiling over $10.6 million in prize money in 2005 alone, but to tee it up alongside the world number one and then give him a three-shot start each and every round wasn't exactly making it any easier.

But in every one of the PGA Tour's myriad statistics categories Poulter's performance revealed a golfer who had yet to adjust to playing week in, week out on the PGA Tour. While he played twice the number of events that he had in 2004, he had missed almost as many cuts as he made and the only top 10 he would register would be in a match play event, the rain-affected World Golf Championships-Accenture Match Play Championship at La Costa in Carlsbad, California.

The stats didn't lie. Off the tee, Poulter lagged at 132nd in the distance category and 107th in terms of accuracy, hitting just 62.28 per cent of fairways. His birdie average, meanwhile, was 3.18 per round, a figure that placed him 173rd on the PGA Tour. Indeed, virtually the only thing to give him some crumb of comfort was that when it came to holing out between three and five feet, he was the PGA Tour leader.

It was a showing that left him with returns of $946,890 and a finish of 86th on the end-of-season money list, and while that was more than adequate for Poulter to keep his Tour card in the United States, it was hardly the brick-through-a-window season he had wanted to have to start his US career in earnest.

In time, Poulter would learn that playing as many events as he could was actually doing more damage to his game than good. In 2012 for example, after a bout of pneumonia, he took six weeks off, albeit enforced, and the break would help enormously. Of course, the temptation as a player is to take as many opportunities as you can and follow the money around the globe but as Tiger Woods has proved by cutting his schedule down to around half of the events that most golfers play, there are huge benefits to be had from being more selective. "You have got to take the breaks," Poulter said recently. "You don't realize what it takes out of you when you go gallivanting about around Asia and all over the place, trying to play golf. You can't do it every week if you are slightly tired. You have to be switched on and ready to go… It's a lesson to learn. Take some time off, stay fresh."

But while 2005 had been winless, it was patently obvious that Poulter was still trying to acclimatize to a period in his professional life that had never been busier. It is, of course, the flip-side of success, especially in golf. The more tournaments you win, the more in demand you become. Couple that with a look and an attitude that was largely alien to the world of golf and you have a player who is not only interesting and popular but inherently marketable too.

Certainly, the comparative inconsistency of 2005 hadn't dissuaded potential sponsors from working with Poulter and in January 2006, he signed a new equipment deal with Cobra Golf, the California-based manufacturer. Formed in 1973 by the Australian amateur Tom Crow (and now a subsidiary of the German sportswear giant Puma), Cobra previously had the likes of triple-US Open winner Hale Irwin and Beth Daniel, a 33-time winner on the LPGA Tour on their books. Crucially, back in 1991 they had managed to persuade one of golf's biggest stars, the Australian Greg Norman, to be one of their endorsers, giving him an equity stake in the company, an opportunity to assist in the design of their clubs and a chance to own Cobra's distribution arm back in Australia, rather than pay the many millions of dollars that it would ordinarily have cost them in a straight cash deal.

Now, Cobra had earmarked Poulter as part of their wider strategy to re-establish themselves in modern-day Tour golf and one that also saw them enlist other professionals like the Australian Geoff Ogilvy, the Colombian star Camilo Villegas, Americans JB Holmes and Kevin Na and the LPGA Tour's Jeong Jang.

It would prove to be a successful switch for some of the players. With the ink still drying on the contracts, PGA Tour rookie Holmes won February's FBR Open in Phoenix in just his fourth start on the main tour, hotly pursued by Villegas in second place. Three weeks later, Ogilvy won the WGC-Accenture Match Play Championship at La Costa, before taking his maiden major title when he won the toughest major of them all, the US Open Championship, at Winged Foot in Mamaroneck, New York, a victory that would propel him up the world rankings from number 50 to a career-high number eight.

The question, now, of course, was whether the change to Cobra would yield similarly dramatic results for Ian Poulter's game. Initially, the signs were promising. At the Abu Dhabi Golf Championship in late January, Poulter took a tie for 10th and there was also tie for sixth at the Johnnie Walker Classic in Perth, Australia. But while matters looked to be heading in the right direction, there was another storm brewing and one that, with the benefit of hindsight, he could surely have avoided.

While in Abu Dhabi, Poulter had opted to play his third round not in one of his typically cutting-edge shirts but in a replica shirt of his beloved Arsenal. Having recently come to the end of a clothing deal with adidas, he was now free to wear whatever he wanted to on the golf course, which, for the Abu Dhabi Championship at least happened to be the commemorative Arsenal Centenary shirt in redcurrant. Thankfully, though, he refrained from going the whole hog and donning the shorts and socks.

But his choice of clothing caused consternation from the Tour and having been summoned over by the tournament director David Garland, he was told that it did not comply with Tour regulation on dress codes, a point that Poulter disputed. "I can't see any problem with the shirt. It has a collar and I am not being paid to wear it, nor do I have a contract to wear it," he explained later. "Yes, it has got an Arsenal club badge and yes, it does have the O2 sponsorship, but I am not reaping any reward from it. At the moment I don't have a clothing contract and can wear whatever the hell I want. There is a rule about the size of a logo, but only if you are sponsored and being paid by that company, and that's where we differ. I haven't got a problem, but it seems the Tour might have and if they have, they can tell me not to wear it and I won't wear it."

Of course, he could have dismissed the incident as being little more than the actions of a passionate golfer who always wore his heart on his sleeve, but as Poulter had opted for the short-sleeved version he didn't really have any sleeves to blame it on. Besides, as football kits go, it wasn't particularly offensive, and, indeed, it wasn't the style or the cut of the shirt that irked the European Tour. It was the enormous logo for the telecommunications company O2 emblazoned right across the chest that had turned the Tour's commercial heads, not least because O2 wasn't one of the Tour's official partners.

Two weeks later, Poulter arrived in Dubai for the Desert Classic, and told the press that not only could he not really see what all the fuss had been about but that he now had four more Arsenal shirts in his case (all with suitably smaller logos) and that he fully intended on wearing at least one of them during the competition.

If it seemed as if he was deliberately pushing boundaries then that was because he was. Though he knew it could land him in trouble, the ever-playful Poulter knew only too well the publicity that could and would be generated by such a simple gesture. Indeed, as far as he was concerned, there was only one thing in life worse than being talked about and that was *not* being talked about. Besides, most pay-and-play municipal courses in the UK wouldn't allow someone on the course wearing a football shirt, so the idea that Poulter could wear what he wanted in some of professional golf's most prestigious tournaments seemed to be deliberately provocative. Even his own club, Woburn, was forced to come out and issue a statement on the matter. "If Ian were to come here wearing a football shirt, we'd impose the same rules on him that we do to anybody else," said the club's Richard Corbett.

A meeting of the European Tour players' committee would be convened in Dubai, where among the topics for discussion would be Poulter's latest fashion statement. The verdict was swift in coming and while they decided that Poulter did not need to be fined for his choice of shirt in Abu Dhabi, the wearing of football kits during tournament play would now be outlawed for all players.

Four years later, in an interview with me, Poulter would admit that he knew he had been pushing his luck by playing in his club's colours. "I was just trying to push the envelope a bit. You have to try, don't you?" he shrugged. "Mind you, they changed the rules straight after that and banned players from wearing football shirts so it didn't do much good."

It wouldn't be the first time that year that his love for Arsenal would interfere with his day job. Later, in mid-May, Poulter found himself in the unusual position of desperately trying to find a way to engineer a trip to the Stade de France in Paris to see his club play in their first ever Champions League Final. Manager Arsène Wenger's team had surprised everyone by beating the likes of Ajax, Real Madrid and Juventus on their way to a final date against another of European football's superpowers, Barcelona. Inconsiderately, though, European football's governing body UEFA had chosen to organize the fixture without first consulting Poulter's schedule, and while the Arsenal squad were preparing for the club's biggest ever game in Paris, Poulter was otherwise engaged at the Irish Open at County Kildare's Carton House.

With the game set for the Wednesday evening and Poulter off as an early starter on Thursday morning, there seemed to be no way that he could get to France and back in time for his first round. But desperate times called for desperate measures. So after fulfilling his duties in Wednesday's pro-am tournament – sponsors take a dim view of players dropping out of these events – he decided to charter a seven-seater private jet from Dublin to take himself, his dad Terry, fellow golfer (and Gooner) Simon Khan and some friends over to France, getting him to the stadium just in time for the kick-off.

To his delight, Arsenal, without their goalkeeper Jens Lehmann, who had been sent off after just 18 minutes, would even take the lead in the game as the central defender Sol Campbell headed home just before the half-time interval. But the Gunners' lead would be short-lived. After the break, Arsenal seemed to run out of gas and after Samuel Eto'o drew the sides level in the 76th minute, it seemed as if there was only going to be one winner. Sure enough, the decisive goal would come five minutes later when the substitute Juliano Belletti slipped the ball through Almunia's legs to win it for the Catalan giants and crush Arsenal's resistance – and Poulter's dreams.

The game over, Poulter and his party then jumped in the car they had waiting outside the stadium to whisk them to the airport, arriving back in the early hours of Thursday morning with just enough time to grab a couple of hours' sleep before his tee-off. It had been an expensive night and, ultimately, a fruitless one for Poulter and Arsenal and what he patently didn't need after such a whirlwind day and dizzy night was a long, drawn-out round of golf.

That, though, was exactly what he got. Although he made his 7.50am tee time as planned, a bleary-eyed Poulter then had to endure a six-hour delay during his round as gale-force winds lashed Carton House, even moving the golf balls as they sat on some of the more exposed putting surfaces on the Colin Montgomerie-designed course. At the par-three 17th, for example, a sudden gust blew his 10-foot putt racing past the flag. Then, seconds later, another freak gust blew the ball completely off the green. "I had to chip it back onto the green," shrugged Poulter later.

The net result was that Poulter would finish his first round more than 12 hours after he first teed off. "That was bizarre, really," he said. "I didn't anticipate spending more than 12 hours to complete my round of golf. Unbelievable. It was certainly quicker to jump on a plane to Paris, watch the game, come back and go to bed. All in all, on a couple of hours' sleep, I am more than happy to shoot one under in those conditions."

It was indeed a fine round of golf given the circumstances and put Poulter in a strong position to land his first title since 2004. But a week that had started so promisingly – on the golf course at least – would end in more controversy for Poulter. Whether it was some residual disappointment from seeing his favourite team beaten in the biggest match in their history or the fact that the conditions had made playing almost impossible is unclear, but Poulter's mood darkened as the tournament progressed.

After the promise of the first two rounds, he was still in contention after Saturday's third round when a one-over-par 73 left him just three shots adrift of the leaders Thomas Bjorn, Paul Casey and Anthony Wall. But what happened in the final round (held over to Monday because of torrential rain) was simply bewildering as an 85 – the worst round of the day – sent Poulter spiralling down the leaderboard to end in a tie for 60th place.

But if the round itself was shocking by Poulter's standards, it would be compounded by an incident that would once more land him in hot water with the European Tour. As he looked for his ball in the rough during that final round, his frustration had boiled over and he began swearing at one of the marshals who was actually trying to help him find his ball. Though he thought nothing of it at the time, the incident would be reported to the European Tour and, again, Poulter had some explaining to do.

Summoned by the Tour's chief executive George O'Grady to meet him at the following week's BMW Championship at Wentworth, Poulter apologized for his actions and, on his own suggestion, was given the opportunity to set the level of his fine. Poulter and O'Grady would settle on £5,000, equalling the highest fine ever dished out by the European Tour and effectively wiping out the €5,610 he had won at the Irish Open.

For his part, O'Grady was now happy that Poulter had apologized to the marshals in Ireland and that the case, as far as he was concerned, was now closed. "I tend to feel there's much, much more good in Ian Poulter than one particular loss of temper in very tough conditions," he explained. "He's a good role model most of the time. One incident has been dealt with now and that's it – it's just a blip. His record book is now clear. He's apologized, been fined, now we move on. He's a hard professional sportsman in a tough game. These things are going to happen from time to time. We're in the real world."

That "real world", however, wasn't such a great place for Poulter, at least professionally. At the prestigious BMW PGA Championship – the European Tour's flagship event – he had started solidly, a three-under-par 69 leaving him in a tie for ninth place, just a couple of shots shy of the leaders. Come Friday, however, Poulter's form around the famous West Course deserted him just as the rest of the field pulled away and a 78 would see him at a loose end for the weekend.

Since his first appearance at the then Volvo PGA Championship in 2000, Poulter had never really found Wentworth to his liking, with a succession of missed cuts and a highest finish of a tie for 33rd in 2005 all he really had to show for his efforts around the West Course. In time, though, his apparent dislike – disdain even – for the course would intensify, especially after the 2002 Open champion (and Wentworth Estate resident) Ernie Els had been hired to tweak the design.

Between 2005 and 2012 the South African would undertake an ambitious redesign of Harry Colt's original layout, reviewing and remodelling all of the greenside and fairway bunkers and installing 18 new greens too. The chief difference, however, would come at the par-five 18th, a hole which had long since become an almost guaranteed birdie for most professionals. Now, instead of a relatively straightforward second shot into the green, there would be a new, snaking brook installed in front of the putting surface, designed to snare those approaches that were anything less than spot-on. It was now a classic risk-and-reward hole.

While it looked as pretty as a picture, the remodelling hadn't exactly met with universal approval, largely because this celebrated club in Surrey's stockbroker belt didn't look particularly English any more. The European Ryder Cup star Paul Casey, for instance, argued that like historic buildings, certain golf courses should be protected from any redevelopments that weren't in keeping with the original design. The *Telegraph's* Mark Reason, meanwhile, labelled the hole a "ghastly sell-out" and "a nasty piece of Americana", maintaining, "The result is something that looks flash, but is golfing nonsense… They spent half a million quid on an aquatic folly – there goes the winner, not waving, but drowning."

Poulter too would take exception to the new closing hole. In 2011, for instance, he had finished his second round with a double-bogey at the 18th and walked off the course "absolutely fuming". Never the longest of drivers, his strategy for the new hole was to lay up short of the brook before hitting a little wedge into the green. But it didn't work out that way. "I've hit what I thought was a perfect third shot, maybe caught out a tiny bit by the wind, and it pitches by the green and finishes in the hazard," he huffed. "Marvellous!"

Later, Poulter would be more strident in his critique of Els' new design. "The tees, the fairways, the rough, the greens, and those 20-foot-deep bunkers," he ranted. "I don't like this golf course, period. End of story."

While it was one thing criticizing the likes of Colin Montgomerie for some of his course designs, Poulter should have known that it was a different matter entirely starting a slanging match with someone as tough-talking and no-nonsense as Ernie Els. "A guy double-bogeys the last hole [because] he doesn't hit the right shot, and then he blames the golf course for his bad shots," said The Big Easy. "I don't take that lightly. We'll have a word when it's suitable, when he's calmed down a little bit. He's done a lot of damage to the flagship event. He's a Ryder Cup player, and to come out with things like that is uncalled for. He should think twice when he does that."

But if it sounded ominous, as if Els would soon be cornering him in the locker room to put his point across a little more forcefully, man to man perhaps, then Poulter was unrepentant. "I'll speak freely," he insisted, as though he were a fearless pro-democracy campaigner bravely waging war against some despotic regime. "Many others will not."

Though the 2011 version of Ian Poulter was more confident and assured than he may have been in 2006, he was still, ostensibly, the same free spirit he had always been. The difference was that, now an established professional with sufficient tournament wins and significant Ryder Cup experience under his belt, he felt more than entitled to express his opinions where once he may have been simply laughed off as the guy with the crazy haircut and even crazier trousers. In that respect, it made Poulter something of an anomaly in the game, a player who rather than toe the party line and simply praise the course, the sponsors and whoever else had a role to play without ever meaning it, spoke his mind without any fear of the consequences. Not only did it make for good copy for the sports press but it made a welcome change for the game of professional golf too.

Back in 2006, though, it had seemed, increasingly, as though Poulter was playing his best golf not in his own backyard but on the golden fairways of the United States and its PGA Tour. Whether it was the weather or the rewards on offer, it seemed that when he teed it up Stateside, things just seemed to click. A quick examination of the finishes he enjoyed in the early summer that year show a player who was capable of finishing tied seventh at the Zurich Classic in New Orleans, tied ninth at the Barclays and tied 12th at the US Open at a fiendishly difficult Winged Foot, but whose consistency on the other side of the pond left a lot to be desired. Take the month of July, where one week he would take a tie for third at the French Open, only to follow it with a finish of 52nd at the Smurfit Kappa European Open at the K Club in Ireland the next. One week, he could be a model of consistency at the Scottish Open at Loch Lomond, shooting a 67 and three rounds of 70 to tie for 14th, the next week he was crumbling to rounds of 75 and 76 to miss the cut at the Open Championship at the Royal Liverpool Golf Club, Hoylake.

It was a maddening and mystifying run and one that Poulter seemed to be at a loss to address. But it wasn't a crisis, not really. After all, those three finishes in the US had helped him bank nearly half a million dollars, a return that more than made up for the couple of thousand pounds he got for effectively just turning up at Royal Liverpool.

But that Open Championship was one of those tournaments that gave grist to the mill of all of Poulter's detractors. For one so often criticized for being more style than substance (and the definition of "style" is obviously subjective), Poulter's predilection to hog the headlines often backfired on him. At St Andrews for the 134th Open, Poulter had, for example, turned up for his first round in his infamous Claret Jug trousers.

But after some of the shocking strides he had revealed in previous years, Poulter outdid himself at Hoylake, where he emerged for his first round wearing an outfit that made it look as if he'd come straight from a shift at TGI Fridays. With a red visor on his head, he sported a white shirt with a Union Jack design across his chest and shoulders, and teamed it with a red pair of sequined slacks with white piping, replete with sparkling Claret Jug design low on the leg.

Public reaction to Poulter's latest catwalk appearance was mixed at best. With a hint of the Elvis and maybe a little homage to Evel Knievel too, Poulter's look attracted several wolf whistles as he made his way round Royal Liverpool and also caught the eye of Seve Ballesteros, who had cut him down to size with *that* quip at St Andrews a year earlier, and who was now his playing partner for the first two rounds. "He looks to me like a Spanish matador," said Seve, who had opted for a simple but stylish white shirt and dark trousers. "But he should not be in red, because the bull always goes for red."

With security reassuringly tight at Hoylake the chances of any bulls rampaging through the course were slim, but for all his sartorial statements, Poulter still found himself lagging behind the 49-year-old Ballesteros, winding up one shot worse off than his playing partner with a three-over-par total of 75.

The following day, Poulter would opt for something a little more conservative (if such a word existed in his vocabulary). Now he was dressed, Gary Player-esque, in all black, with only some sequins around the collars, pockets and seams to break up the gloom. It was part *Strictly Come Dancing*, part frontier town sheriff, but it would be Hoylake that would head him off at the pass, driving him out of town at the halfway stage, a second-round 76 leaving him just four places off the tail end of the leaderboard in a tie for 136th.

The lesson, it seemed, was clear: if you're going to talk the talk, you'd better be good enough to walk the walk. More galling, though, was the deleterious effect that his Open showing would have on his chance of qualifying for Ian Woosnam's European Ryder Cup team for the match against the United States at the K Club in Ireland in late September.

Having been part of the team in 2004, when Bernhard Langer's Europe dismantled Hal Sutton's side at Oakland Hills, Poulter had made the Ryder Cup a focal point of his season but the late charge he had mounted to make the 2004 team two years earlier had failed to materialize when he needed it most. At the last event to count toward qualification, the BMW International Open in Munich, Germany – the same event where he had mounted that irresistible surge to squeeze into the team in 2004 – Poulter's Ryder Cup hopes died not with a bang but with a whimper. Two rounds of 76 and 70 would see him miss the cut by three shots and any lingering chance he may have had to qualify for the team, or at the very least plant a seed in the mind of captain Woosnam for his wild card selections, disappeared in the space of two soul-sapping rounds.

Yet it wasn't the performance at the BMW that had done for Poulter's chances, nor was it the missed cut at Hoylake in the Open Championship, even though that had thrown an almighty spanner into his plans. All it was, put simply, was a gnawing inconsistency and an irritating inability to prolong those periods of good form that he found himself in. It was the difference between being a really good golfer and a great one.

Despite some gutsy performances, including a tie for ninth at the PGA Championship at Medinah Country Club and a tie for 13th at the WGC-Bridgestone Invitational at Firestone, Poulter had left his challenge to stake a genuine claim for a place in the European team for the K Club far too late. Now, there were too many candidates ahead of him in the pecking order and with his world ranking now in the 50s, and falling, it wouldn't be difficult for Woosnam to look elsewhere.

Certainly, missing out on the K Club had been like a rapier to the heart for Poulter. "Of course I was gutted," he told *Golf Punk* magazine in 2007. "The 2004 Ryder Cup is the greatest sporting moment of my life – it's difficult to describe. I'm getting goose-bumps and smiling just thinking about it. But last year I made a decision to play more in America to test myself at a new level. I don't want to sound disrespectful to the European Tour, but the fields I play in America are stronger every week. The bottom line is I just didn't play well enough last year, anywhere. And had I played well enough, it wouldn't have mattered where it was, because I'd have got into the team. And though I was disappointed, I know I'm a better player for the experience."

What made it all the more difficult to stomach was that it would be a Ryder Cup to remember (not that any are really forgettable). Propelled ever onwards by an ineffably gutsy and almost superhuman performance by Darren Clarke, they had torn Tom Lehman's American team asunder and equalled the record-breaking 18½–9½ victory that Poulter and his team-mates had recorded at Oakland Hills, two years earlier.

Clarke had been a colossus. Just weeks after his wife Heather lost her battle with cancer, he had taken up Ian Woosnam's offer of a captain's pick, even though he hadn't picked up a club for nearly two months. Cheered on by a partisan crown in Straffan, he won all three of the games he had played in, breaking down in tears on the 16th green when he defeated Zach Johnson in the singles on Sunday. It had been a display that defied the odds. Even the American team ringing the 16th green stood and applauded his effort, with Tom Lehman and Tiger Woods leading the way. With tears streaming down his ruddy face, Clarke had been embraced by his captain, who held his arm aloft like a prizefighter at the end of a long, brutal bout.

Yes, there were tears, cheers and quite a few beers after the most emotionally-charged Ryder Cup in history – and Poulter hadn't been a part of it. It was something that he was determined to ensure wouldn't happen again.

Poulter's frustration was doubtless compounded by the fact that he was also now in the kind of form that, had he shown earlier in the campaign, would have seen him strolling into the Ryder Cup team. At the Banco Madrid Valle Romano Open in Spain, a week before the Ryder Cup began, his form was so impressive and so exceptional, not only did he amass 24 birdies over the course of the tournament, but he didn't even drop a shot until the 13th hole of his fourth and final round, as he cantered to his first win in two years. Not that a cheque for €166,660 and another nice pot for the trophy cabinet was any consolation for Poulter. "I don't think this win will soften the blow [of not making the team]," he said. "I came here to move up the world rankings and make sure I played in the Amex [the WGC-American Express Championship] and I've achieved that, but I'm still very disappointed not to be playing this week."

With another win under his designer belt and having been forced to sit by and watch as Europe racked up another huge win against the United States at the K Club, it was entirely predictable that Poulter would take his frustration out on the golf course and, for once that year, he did it in the best way possible, not by abusing volunteers or cocking a snook at authority but by playing some sublime golf.

At the WGC-American Express Championship, played back in his old stamping ground in Hertfordshire at The Grove, Poulter more

Above: Rookie pro Poulter celebrates his maiden win on the European Tour at the Italian Open in Cagliari in October 2000. The victory came in just his fourth appearance on the European Tour and helped him to win the Sir Henry Cotton Rookie of the Year award as well.

Left: Poulter's radical blond and red hairstyle caused alarm in some of golf's more conservative clubhouses in 2003. It was outrageous fashion statements like this that certainly helped Poulter, and golf itself, appeal to what was often referred to as the "Golf Punk" generation.

Opposite: After a record 2004 Ryder Cup victory over the United States at Oakland Hills Country Club in Michigan, Poulter leads the European celebrations. Just 11 years earlier he had been on the other side of the ropes, attending the Ryder Cup as a spectator and camping in a field nearby.

Above: Poulter celebrates with his daughter Aimee-Leigh after defeating Sergio Garcia in a play-off at the Volvo Masters at Valderrama in October 2004. The victory maintained his impressive run of winning an event in each of his first five years on the European Tour.

Left: Poulter's choice of leg wear at the 2004 Open Championship at Hoylake garnered more column inches than his golf. The following year, he once more delighted and irritated golf fans in equal measure with his "Claret Jug" trousers at the Open at St Andrews.

Opposite: After Poulter wore an Arsenal football shirt at the Abu Dhabi Championship in January 2006, the European Tour changed the rules governing the wearing of replica shirts during tournament play.

Above: Poulter bags an ace at the 16th hole during the opening round of the Masters at Augusta in April 2008. It was the first hole-in-one at the Masters in three years, a feat described by Poulter at the time as "the biggest adrenaline rush I've ever had".

Opposite: Poulter was a controversial captain's pick for Nick Faldo's Ryder Cup team at Valhalla Golf Club, Kentucky, in September 2008, but his four points from five games more than justified Faldo's faith in him.

Above: Poulter and his Ryder Cup colleague Graeme McDowell revel in another famous Ryder Cup victory after the Irishman secured the all-important point at Celtic Manor, Wales, in October 2010. Once more, Poulter was in fine form, returning three points out of four as Europe snatched a dramatic 14½–13½ win.

Left: A key win came for Poulter at the WGC-Accenture Matchplay Championship at Arizona's Ritz-Carlton Golf Club in February 2010 where he bagged $1.4 million, the biggest cheque of his professional career.

Left: Poulter and his best friend on tour, Justin Rose, hit the bubbly after the "Miracle of Medinah" Ryder Cup win in 2012. It was a special moment for the pair and showed just how far both had come since they used to room together on the Challenge Tour.

Below: Poulter walks with his children Aimee-Leigh (right) and Luke during the Par Three Contest prior to the 2010 Masters. He went on to finish the tournament in a tie for 10th place.

than proved he had the game and the appetite to mix it with the world's best players. And while Tiger Woods won by eight shots – he always did – Poulter came home in a tie for second, ahead of all 21 of the Ryder Cup players who were in the field that week.

And if it seemed like he was trying to prove a point, that's because he was.

Chapter 6
Talking the Talk

@IanJamesPoulter *Some of you w****** make me laugh. Blocking a lot this afternoon. Your (sic) all big behind your smart phones & keyboards*

In response to criticism of his performance at the 2013 Masters, where Poulter missed the cut

The polar worlds of golf and fashion have always endured, rather than enjoyed, an uneasy relationship over the years. From the safe slacks and sometimes dubious knitwear of the professional ranks to the wholly unimaginative default Chinos and polo shirt combination of the weekend hacker, golf has all too often been the sport that fashion didn't just forget, but bypassed entirely.

It's hardly surprising really. Here, after all, is a game played for the most part by white, middle-class men, a demographic not exactly known for their style nous. All of which made Ian Poulter's forays into more fashionable golf clothing intriguing. Irrespective of what you actually thought of his dress sense and whether it was in any way appropriate for a game as naturally conservative as golf, the fact that people were talking about it was a clear sign that change was afoot. Poulter wasn't alone. There were also new fashion labels trying their hand at golfwear too, all of which seemed to appeal to a younger, more style-conscious audience who just wanted to take to the fairways without looking like the comedian Ronnie Corbett. The Swedish designer Johan Lindeberg, for example, won many awards for his cutting-edge ranges, dressing Swedish professionals like Freddie Jacobson and Jesper Parnevik.

The trend toward more stylish golf clothing seemed to be part of a wider movement, one in which a new wave of younger golfers were being drawn into the game, tempted to try it because of the effect Tiger Woods and his global domination had had on the general perception of the sport. This went hand in hand with the launch of a new title into the golf magazine market in 2004. Billed as "The golf mag for the rest of us", *Golf Punk* was less concerned with the intricacies and technicalities of the golf swing and more focused on the inherent joy of a round of golf, whatever the reader's handicap. It was fresher, funnier and more fashionable than the existing titles, as the magazine's publisher Danny Crouch explains. "*Golf Punk* magazine was – amongst many other things – a pioneering golf publication for fashion brands, championing an attitude that saw J.Lindeberg, Tommy Hilfiger and Hugo Boss all launch campaigns to promote their new golf specific ranges. But whilst each brand had their own tour playing ambassadors – Jesper Parnevik, Nick Dougherty and Martin Kaymer respectively – it was Ian Poulter that transcended the golf media and broke into the mainstream as the figurehead for golf's modern new style."

It's a view reinforced by the magazine's founder and editor-in-chief, Tim Southwell, who, in Ian Poulter, found the living embodiment of the very ethos of the magazine. "He was one of the first golfers who looked like they had an interesting life outside of the ropes. He was trailblazing in his approach to fashion on the fairways, bringing an element of style and fun to the game,

increasing interest and drawing in a younger audience," he explains.
"Suddenly golf was on the back and front pages. Ian was a perfect
poster boy for *Golf Punk* and it wasn't long after our launch that he
was on the front cover. Since then Ian has elevated his golf game
dramatically and is now one of the best – and best dressed – golfers
in the world."

In time, Poulter would become a regular fixture in *Golf Punk*
and, for that matter, the remaining golf publications, all of whom
were suddenly keen to show just how "down with the kids" they
really were. In the April 2007 edition of the magazine, Poulter
showed off his barn conversion near Bletchley in Buckinghamshire.
It was an interesting snapshot of a golfer on the verge of great
things. The trappings of his not inconsiderable success to date were
there for the readers to see – the BMWs in the driveway, the Ford
GT40 in the garden, the signed and personalized Pelé shirt and
the snooker table that his friend Ronnie O'Sullivan won the 2004
World Championship on – but what did come across was Poulter's
determination to try and balance the apparently irreconcilable
demands of professional golf on the one hand and a normal family
life on the other. This, remember, was a man still wracked by guilt for
missing the birth of his son as he was stuck in an airport terminal in
Germany. "It can be a pain in the arse sometimes," he shrugged. "It's
not the actual travelling but the time away from home. I can occupy
myself by socializing with Justin Rose, Clarkey and Adam Scott
when I'm in Orlando, but it's the time that gets you, really. I love
my family and love being at home, watching cartoons with the kids,
seeing them develop in front of me. I'm lucky that I'm privileged
enough to be able to provide them with the things that my parents
couldn't afford, and to see them enjoy these things is wonderful. But

I want to make sure they're raised well and become good people. At the end of the day, being called 'Daddy' every morning is far more important than winning golf tournaments."

For Poulter, professional golf and the riches it promised was also a way to further his interests off the golf course and not just in a material sense. Here was an opportunity for him to develop his own ideas for business and to push the Poulter brand in new and interesting directions. Of course, there were precedents of sorts within the game, most notably in the shape of the Australian double-major winner Greg Norman, whose success on the golf course helped spawn a global business empire that encompassed everything from clothing ranges to vineyards and restaurants, in addition to more typical golfing pursuits such as course design and tournament and event management. Certainly, the way in which Norman had used his entrepreneurial skills appealed to Poulter. "You only have to look at Greg Norman and the success he's had away from the fairways. Obviously he was number one in the world and that must have made the transition easier. But I have a strong work ethic, coupled with a vision of where I see myself in the future – I want to be as successful as possible off the golf course."

Given his burgeoning reputation for being the Tour's premier trendsetter, it was almost inevitable that Poulter would decide to branch out and launch his own range of clothing, and in 2007, with the help of a reported £1 million investment, IJP Design was born. For years, Poulter had been sketching his own clothing designs as he traversed the globe: on airline coasters, letterheads and those complimentary writing pads you get in hotels but never seem to use. But with his profile now higher than it had ever been, it seemed like an entirely natural and obvious diversification for him, even though the easier option would have been to sign a new, seven-figure deal with adidas, Puma or any other of the big sportswear manufacturers.

As a player known for his trousers, Poulter's brand philosophy focused on designing the trousers first and then co-ordinating the rest of a player's outfit around them. "Leading with the legs," he called it. The initial collection would feature a range of tartan trousers – all licensed by the Scottish Tartan Authority – and, as Poulter once explained to me, it was part and parcel of his belief that to play well you needed to look and feel good too. "Historically, golf and fashion have never seen eye to eye," he said. "Personally, I think it's too easy for people to just throw a pair of khaki trousers on with a polo shirt. It takes some thought and some effort to look good but I think it's worth it. My signature trouser is the boot cut, which I've been wearing for a while now, especially the tartan one. They're like an anti-Parnevik trouser. He does like a drainpipe, does Jesper."

Poulter's designs harked back to a time when golf clothing was stylish and unashamedly out there, as the likes of Jack Nicklaus, Arnold Palmer and Johnny Miller strode the fairways in the kind of outfits that were part comedy golfer and part pimp. "They were wearing tartan trousers and bright colours, flat-fronted trousers, slightly bootlegged at the bottom, funky shoes with flaps, and shirts with big collars. It was a cool look. And it was fun," says Poulter. "Why can't we get back to how it was back then?"

It wasn't just the stars of yesteryear that had inspired Poulter's collection. Modern-day players like the late Payne Stewart had also influenced the way he dressed on the golf course; he would even wear plus-fours as a mark of respect for the 1999 US Open champion. "The game misses him. He was a character. And he could play, too. This sport needs characters, like John McEnroe was to tennis," he added. "Golf often gets criticized for being bland. Well, if you wear khaki trousers and a boring coloured top, then you don't always look good on the course. But, if you look down the range these days, people are starting to take care and trying to change."

That clothes are important to who Ian Poulter is goes without saying and while he could have a team of stylists carefully planning and co-ordinating what he wears for each and every tournament he plays in, he prefers to stand or fall by his own decisions. "Nobody tells me what to wear," he once said.

A giant dressing room in his new house in Orlando, meanwhile, is testament to how much time and effort he puts into his appearance. There, you'll find endless rails of clothes in all manner of styles and materials and all of them perfectly and uniformly spaced from each other. There are three drawers that contain his belts and a glass cabinet housing his 42 watches, although quite why you would need 42 watches is a debate for another day.

Increasingly, though, Poulter's aspirations away from the golf course seemed eminently sensible. He'd never been the type of golfer to struggle by, season by season, worrying about whether he was going to keep his card. He was a golfer who would not only refuse to entertain any thoughts of failure but was always thinking, and planning ahead, as the golf writer Lawrence Donegan explains. "He may not be academically gifted but he is incredibly savvy and possesses an almost intuitive sense of what to say and do in any given situation," he says. "And that will carry him and his brand a very long way."

And with his new business off and running, Poulter was already setting his sights on those players he felt needed a makeover. "I would love to dress Tiger for a week," he said. "I'd have him rocking the old gear – flat caps, plus-fours, the works. He's such an athlete that he could wear anything and look good in it, even a sack or a bin bag. We'd probably all benefit if he started using the old sticks as well."

While it was a nice idea in principle, the likelihood of that happening was remote, not least because Woods hadn't exactly warmed to Poulter's presence on the PGA Tour. It wasn't that there was any real enmity between the pair – their relationship was always cordial – but there seemed to be parts of Poulter's character that, for a while at least, got under the skin of the world's best player. A case in point is an incident that reportedly took place a couple of weeks ahead of the US Open at Pennsylvania's Oakmont Country Club in early June. According to his then coach, Hank Haney, Woods, Poulter and a number of other players had arrived at Oakmont after the Memorial Tournament in Colombus, Ohio, in order to get some practice rounds in ahead of the year's second major. When Poulter realized that Woods, a near neighbour of his in Orlando, was there he came straight out and asked him, "How are we getting home?", knowing full well that Woods would be taking his private jet back to Florida.

Though Woods brushed the Englishman off, thinking no more of it, when he arrived at the airport at the end of the day there was Poulter waiting for a ride home. On board the plane, meanwhile, Woods kicked back in the seats at the front and listened to music, leaving Hank Haney to chat with Poulter. But as the pair talked, Haney's cell phone buzzed into life. It was a text message from Woods up ahead. "Can you believe this dick mooched a ride on my plane?" it said.

The incident, reported in Haney's 2012 book, *The Big Miss*, may have shown an unfamiliar side to Woods, but it was, according to

Haney, part of a natural disdain for players who Woods perceived as
brash or arrogant, especially when they didn't have a track record to
back up their more extravagant claims. While Woods would take a
tie for second at Oakmont, losing out by a single shot to the barrel-
chested Argentinian Angel Cabrera, Poulter's performance would be
solid if unspectacular, a tie for 36th (a total of 18-over par), earning
prize money of $37,000.

But the time had also come for a change of caddie and in 2007
Poulter opted to hire a new bagman, Terry Mundy. With over
20 years' experience, Mundy had spent seven years working with
Britain's most successful female golfer of all time, Laura Davies, and
as the husband of the LPGA Tour player, Johanna Head, had also
worked with a number of players on the women's circuit. Certainly,
he came highly recommended and his ability as a caddie was well
known in the men's game too, as Luke Donald explained. "Terry
used to carry on the women's tour and he was on the bag for one of
the best Asian players. But he got bored with her because she was so
good. He wanted to challenge himself to prove that he could make a
difference. So he chose a player who was way down on the rankings
and brought her up to number 10 on the money-list. After he left
her, she fell back to number 100."

Time would tell whether having Terry on his bag would prove
to be a sound decision for Poulter, but for now it seemed like
a positive change and one that was badly needed. Increasingly,
though, there were signs that Ian was having some problems in
negotiating the many and various demands that were encroaching
on his time. At Jack Nicklaus's Memorial Tournament in early June
he was disqualified after his second round for signing an incorrect
scorecard (he had signed for a three on the par-three 12th when

he actually made a four), while a fit of pique at the Mercedes-Benz Championship in Cologne, Germany, found him in further trouble.

Reaching the par-three 16th, Poulter's wayward tee shot left him so irate that he flipped, taking his five-iron and smashing the marker on the tee box. The incident would cost him another fine, this time undisclosed, from the European Tour. Poulter, however, was unrepentant and as far as he was concerned, the tee marker was just collateral damage. "If anyone gets angry on the course and does something silly then the Tour are going to do what they do," he explained. "If I want to let a bit of my passion show – and I certainly don't want to lose any of my passion for the game – then unfortunately I have to pay for it in the pocket. It doesn't happen every week, but it's part of my make-up. I'm not the sort of person who can play a bad shot and smile, everybody's DNA is different. But it's not as if I've taken a samurai sword and chopped a few heads off."

Indeed. But you could perhaps excuse Poulter's latest outburst. After all, the guy had a lot on his plate, what with his flourishing fashion business and the not insignificant matter of his marriage to Katie; he would miss the Seve Trophy at The Heritage Golf & Spa Resort in Ireland to wed the girl he had met in a Luton disco all those years ago. Doing away with the traditional gift list – it would only have had Ferraris on it anyway – the happy couple asked guests and well-wishers to make donations to two charities: the Willow Foundation, which provides special days for seriously ill 16- to 40-year-olds and to DreamFlight, an organization that takes disabled and seriously ill children on trips to Orlando.

The ceremony, meanwhile, would be held in Woburn Abbey's elegant Sculpture Gallery. Dennis Hopper, Poulter's partner in the

Dunhill Links, flew in from Los Angeles to join in the celebrations, while his close friend Jonathan Spooner, aka DJ Spoony, spun some tunes at the reception. Strangely, though, Poulter, so often a picture of unabashed confidence, felt the occasion got to him and the prospect of standing up and speaking to his nearest and dearest seemed more frightening than the 17th at Sawgrass. "I wasn't born to make public speeches," he said later. "I might look different on TV, but it's nice to have a little barrier there. You know, I am still the same guy I was when I was working in a pro shop, and I have kept all my old friends. There were people at my wedding that I hadn't seen for years and they said that I hadn't changed a bit – that's nice to know."

Scorecards, spats and smashed tee markers aside, it had been a successful year for Poulter. He was one of only seven players in the season to make all four cuts in the majors (and recorded his best finish – 13th – at the Masters), he had five top-10s on the PGA Tour and four top-10s on the European Tour. Fittingly, he would also end the year by winning his final stroke play event, heading the pack at the Dunlop Phoenix Open in Japan to record his ninth worldwide victory. "It's a lovely feeling to win again, and it's so nice to come and do it in Japan," he said. "I have played very steady all year. I've felt comfortable all week. It would be nice to know exactly why, because if you could do that every week you could get into that winning position every week."

And therein lay Poulter's challenge for the forthcoming 2008 season. While it was clear that he was adapting nicely to the demands of global golf, the question as to whether he had the ability to make that all-important step up to regular Tour winner and major champion still remained to be answered.

You need certain attributes and character traits in order to succeed as a professional golfer. Confidence is critical, self-belief key, and the moment you lose one (or both) of these qualities is the moment you may as well throw the clubs in the garage and turn your attentions to commentating.

It's safe to say that Ian Poulter wasn't exactly lacking in either of those departments. Why else, or indeed *how* else, could anybody get away with wearing some of the outfits that he did, especially if he didn't have the game to back it up? "I've always been confident, and though some people might not like that about me, it's carried me a long way. Playing against those seasoned guys in Florida and on the Hippo Tour was a huge education for me, and it made me realize that I didn't have misplaced belief, that I could step up. It's the same when I joined the European Tour. I had respect for the guys around me – Monty, Faldo, etc. – but I wasn't scared of them, you can't be scared if you want to win golf tournaments."

That fervent, unwavering belief in his own ability, however, would eventually land the player in some hot water. For the most part, of course, Poulter is a journalist's dream. Open, candid and approachable, he says what he thinks and feels, and rarely toes any party line. In that respect, he differs from most players in the professional ranks who'd rather opt for blandness and circumspection lest they incur the wrath of the Tour or their sponsors. "I'm honest in my comments," he once said. "I will say it as it is, and if that upsets people, I'm sorry, I really don't care. I'm trying to be me. I can be politically correct, if people really want me to be. But that's boring. Ninety-five per cent of people err on the side of caution, but I'm just trying to be me. I will give people an honest opinion, and people relate to that. They kind of like it."

In March 2008, he gave an interview to *Golf World* magazine in the UK, appearing naked on the cover, save for a strategically-placed and heavily branded pink and black Cobra golf bag, under the coverline "POULTER LAID BARE – WHY THERE'S A LOT MORE TO ME THAN FANCY PANTS".

Remarkably, though, the photographs would be the least of his worries as attention turned to one particular passage of the piece. "The trouble is, I don't rate anyone else," he said. "Don't get me wrong, I respect everyone who is a professional, but the problem is I know I haven't played to my full potential yet. And when that happens it will just be me and Tiger."

Though the two men were born within 11 days of each other, it was there that comparisons end. Poulter, for example, was the world's 22nd ranked player while Woods had enjoyed year after glorious year as the world number one, rewriting golf's record books as he went along. Poulter had won seven tournaments and no majors while Woods had won 85 career titles and with 13 majors already under his belt, was well on the way to eclipsing Jack Nicklaus's record tally of 18.

It was that apparent gulf, if not in talent then in success, that made Poulter's comments seem all the more extraordinary and the fact that he had yet to make any inroads into the world's top 10, let alone challenge Tiger at the summit, suggested that while he could certainly talk the talk, he couldn't walk the walk. When news of the *Golf World* interview broke, Poulter was playing a practice round ahead of the Dubai Desert Classic. As he made his way down the 18th fairway, he could see the familiar faces of the golfing press pack waiting for him behind the hole. Resisting the temptation to take a club or two too many and send his ball scuttling through them,

Poulter duly finished his round (making birdie at the last) and, rather than head straight for the sanctuary of the locker room, marched over to the assembled throng to field their numerous questions about what he had said, or hadn't said, in the article.

One of the waiting press men was the *Guardian*'s then golf correspondent Lawrence Donegan. "We had all seen the piece and were obviously keen to get Ian's take on it so when he came over he did seem a little bothered by the fact that we were there but fair play to him, he just stood there and answered every single question. Most golfers would have just walked straight past us but not Poulter and what sets him apart, I think, is that he doesn't seem to hold grudges either. The next day it was business as normal with him. He just wasn't phased by it."

As luck (and the small matter of a huge appearance fee) would have it, Tiger Woods would also be in the field at the Emirates Golf Club and when the world number one was quizzed about the gap between him and the world's second best player, Phil Mickelson, Woods couldn't resist a little dig of his own. "I thought Poulter was No. 2," he said.

Off the course, all the talk, from the locker room to the media room, was of Poulter's interview. Some of the more devilish players were even considering walking off the practice range to leave Ian and Tiger alone together whenever they were warming up. Poulter, meanwhile, had gone in to damage limitation mode, desperately trying to explain and justify what he had said and meant. "I've been misquoted," he said. "It was taken out of context."

The interview itself had taken place three months earlier and, according to Poulter, it had been difficult to recall precisely what had or had not been said. "And then you do remember," he explained, "and you have given an answer to a question that is very lengthy and a small piece gets quoted, it gets taken out of context and that's very unfair."

Of course, the perfect riposte for those who had ridiculed Poulter for his comments would have been for him to let his golf do all the talking, but come Sunday, he had struggled to a final-round 76 and had to settle for a tie for 39th place. After a stunning final round of 65, meanwhile, the tournament would be won, inevitably, by Tiger Woods.

The end of the Desert Classic would not signal the end of the fallout from Poulter's *Golf World* interview, however. For weeks afterwards, the issue would continue to rear its head, with everyone apparently taking pot shots at him. The *Mirror*, for example, argued that Poulter had been "humiliated" by his comments which, for the record, couldn't have been further from the truth. Besides, in any other sport, the idea of a performer talking up his chances or his potential is part and parcel of the circus, regardless of whether or not they truly believe in themselves. In Poulter's case, however, you knew that he meant every last word of it, even if he still maintained that he had been quoted out of context. Certainly, some of his friends on Tour, like the Ryder Cup player Paul Casey, knew exactly where he was coming from. "For Ian, he'll tell you exactly what he's thinking," he says. "But if Ian believes that – and he does – then there's no reason why he couldn't get to that spot, because for me it's not about talent, it's about work ethic and belief and the rest of it."

The issue was still live by the time Poulter teed it up at Augusta for his fourth crack at a Green Jacket. Not that he seemed unduly concerned. Besides, he felt at ease at Augusta. Having grown up watching the Masters on television, spellbound by a golf course that was far removed from the game he played in Buckinghamshire, he had long harboured thoughts about one day playing there. Now, he was on the threshold of becoming a regular at Augusta, and what made it all the more special was that it was an opportunity for him to share the love; each time he qualified, he would rent the same house with its own chef and the pretty little lake out the front, about 10 minutes down the road from the course. Here he could invite Terry and Theresa over for the week, maybe his Uncle Phil or a couple of pals from back home as well.

Having his nearest and dearest around served to make an already special experience all the more precious. Even today, almost a decade on from his maiden appearance at Augusta, it's a week that Poulter truly relishes. "For me, it never loses that little extra buzz that you get every single time that you drive down the lane and I'm amazed how good you feel every time they let you through the gate," he says. "I think it's very special to park up, go inside the clubhouse, share your locker with somebody else and sit in the same seat that you've sat in eight or nine times before to have lunch. It's neat to share that with friends and family. You know, I do look back at the days in the club shop and think: 'Wow – it's been a fun little road to Augusta so many years in a row!'"

In 2008, even with the hue and cry of the *Golf World* interview still rumbling on in the background, it seemed as though Poulter was genuinely enjoying himself, even if he could have done without some of the attention he was getting. A first-round 70 – equalling his lowest round at the Masters – was aided by the first hole-in-one at the competition for three years when he struck a perfect nine-iron into the heart of the 16th green and let it feed back down the slope and into the hole. On Friday, meanwhile, he would go one shot better, registering a 69 to leave himself handily placed in a tie for third, three shots adrift of the South African Trevor Immelman (one of Poulter's Lake Nona neighbours).

It was typical of Poulter that, far from derailing his season, the *Golf World* debacle had actually galvanized him after some decidedly indifferent performances coming into the season's first major. Sadly, that initial promise would fade and his challenge was to falter over the weekend as rounds of 75 and 78 dropped him back through the field for an eventual placing of tied 25th.

The bright start and disappointing finish at Augusta would come to typify a steady if unspectacular spring for the Englishman. Yes, he was making cuts with comparative ease, picking off the occasional great round or two, but his scoring was hardly ever of a level to trouble the trophy engravers. But if there was a sense that something was awry with his game then it manifested itself at the US Open at San Diego's Torrey Pines. Having opened with a less than impressive 78, Poulter was level par for his round when he reached the 504-yard, par-four, 12th hole. His problems would begin when a wayward tee shot found the rough on the right. With a wedge in his hand, he took a practice swing and succeeded in excavating an enormous mound of turf. Then, when he actually took his shot, his ball squirted just a few feet forward, barely making the first cut of rough, prompting the kind of red-mist moment that was becoming a little too commonplace in his game.

Striding forward, Poulter raised his club like a lumberjack chopping wood for the winter, before slamming it down into ground with gusto and then storming off, pausing only to give the finger to the divot he had just made. It got worse. His next shot would land short of the green, while the follow-up pitch would leave him in three-putt territory. He would leave the hole irate and with a triple bogey clogging up his scorecard. Though he recovered to par the next hole, a double bogey at the 14th sent his mood spiralling downward once more.

By the 15th, he had had enough. Having missed a six-foot par putt, Poulter lazily backhanded a six-inch tap-in – and missed again. That was that. At seven-over par for the day and 14-over par for the tournament, he decided to call it a day. Turning to his playing partners Paul Casey and Luke Donald, Poulter informed them he was walking in. "He just said he was off so he left us," explained Donald. "He just said goodbye and good luck."

Later, it would transpire that Poulter had a swollen wrist – something he had already taken anti-inflammatories for at the Masters – and it was an injury that had flared up again after a game of tennis against his friend Justin Rose the week before the US Open. Still, the explanation didn't come quick enough and, predictably, some of the sports press were already laying into Poulter for what they perceived as another act of petulance. "People have made wrong assumptions which are fairly hurtful," he told the *Daily Mail*'s Peter Higgs, as he returned to the United Kingdom. "This is the first time I've walked off in my professional career and I'd never say I'm not playing golf any more, throw the towel in and walk in. That's not something I believe in. It's not over until it's over and I always try to the very death. But when you could injure yourself badly, you need to be making an exit before it happens."

Of course, it's true that professional golfers only ever seem to walk off the course prematurely after a double bogey (or worse) or another ball dumped in the lake, and never after they have made a birdie, but at least Poulter had a bona fide excuse. Indeed, the true extent of his injury was revealed when, having made the journey back to Europe, he also pulled out of the BMW International in Munich the following week.

A combination of Poulter's mediocre form and now an injured wrist had put his quest to qualify automatically for the 2008 European Ryder Cup team in real jeopardy. By the time he returned to action at the French Open, Poulter was lying 11th on the world points table and 25th on the European points list, positions which would not get him in Nick Faldo's team for the match at Valhalla in September. Still, though, his form showed little sign of improvement. A tie for 30th at the French Open was followed by a tie for 48th at the European Open at the London Golf Club and a share of 25th place at the Barclays Scottish Open at Loch Lomond. Clearly, something needed to change.

As he made his way to Royal Birkdale for the Open Championship, there was still no indication that Poulter was about to mount a challenge for the game's oldest major. One of the few crumbs of comfort for him and, indeed, the rest of the 156-strong field, was that Tiger Woods wasn't in the field for the week – the world number one was back in Orlando recovering from knee surgery.

With Woods absent, the Open Championship seemed more open than ever but no one could really quite envisage what happened. While Poulter crept along tidily, all the talk was of the 53-year-old veteran Greg Norman, who was rolling back the years with the kind of performance that saw him dominate world golf in the 1980s. With his trademark blond locks flowing in the breeze whipping in from the Irish Sea, the two-time Open champion finished the third round with a two-shot lead over the South

Korean KJ Choi and the reigning champion Padraig Harrington to become the oldest golfer in the history of the event to hold the 54-hole lead.

With everybody's attention distracted by the Great White Shark's assault on his favourite major, Poulter had slipped under the radar and even a third-round 75 hadn't seen him lose any real ground on the leaders. On Sunday, dressed in an ice-white top and pink trousers, he was clearly in the mood to do something special. Starting six shots behind Norman, he exploded into life as the round progressed, playing the last 10 holes in three-under par and when he birdied the 16th, the emotion he showed suggested that he believed he was now in with a genuine chance of landing that elusive first major championship.

While he signed for a 69 to take the clubhouse lead, Poulter's failure to birdie any of the par-five holes – he three-putted the 17th for par, for instance – would prove costly and though he managed to overhaul the overnight leader Greg Norman, he would still finish four shots adrift of Harrington, now a winner of back-to-back Opens.

Still, the fact that he had finally put himself in a position to win a major and had been there at the death when they handed out the trophy imbued him with a new-found confidence. "It was a good experience to be put in that position, to feel like I had a chance to win," he said later. "I felt I performed well down that stretch. Obviously it wasn't to be and Padraig had a fantastic finish. But it is always nice to know that, if you are in that position, under pressure, you can hit the right shots at the right time."

What was equally impressive was Poulter's professionalism after the Open had finished. Though he had just come second, he resisted the temptation to celebrate and headed home. The following day he was booked in at Woburn to give a lesson to a group of children and sure enough, at 9am, there he was, impeccably turned out and eager to please. When duty called in any walk of life, it seemed Poulter could always be relied on, even if he had just nearly won his first major.

But his best ever finish in a major, a runners-up cheque for £450,000 and a shiny silver salver for the trophy cabinet would not just help to bolster Poulter's flagging confidence, it would also boost his chances of making the European team for the 2008 Ryder Cup. Since he made his debut in the event in 2004, Poulter had longed to return and the fact that he had missed out in 2006, when Ian Woosnam's team had won one of the most memorable and comprehensive victories in the competition, continued to irk him.

The issue now was not Poulter's suitability for the Ryder Cup – he was a natural – but whether he could make Nick Faldo's team as of right, rather than rely on being selected as one of the wild card picks. The debate about just who should take Faldo's two places reached fever pitch at the last event to count in the qualifying competition for the European Ryder Cup team, the Johnnie Walker Championship at Gleneagles, not least because Poulter had opted not to play, leaving his place in the hands of fate or, more accurately, Nick Faldo. "I have called Nick Faldo and told him of my decision and hope my performance so far this year will earn one of his two wildcard picks," Poulter explained via a statement issued through the European Tour.

Certainly, Poulter was in a difficult position. Having missed the cut in the opening event of the PGA Tour's FedEx Cup play-offs he had to compete in Boston at the Deutsche Bank Championship to have any chance of making it through to the final two events, the BMW Championship and the Tour Championship. It was, moreover, his only chance to make up the 15 events he had to play on the PGA Tour to maintain his membership. It was a conflict of interests that he struggled to reconcile, but when he made his decision ahead of Gleneagles, it provoked some surprise and, in the case of one particular player, something verging on outrage.

As he endeavoured to prolong his proud record of playing in every Ryder Cup since his debut at Kiawah Island in 1991, Scotland's Colin Montgomerie was less than enamoured by Poulter's decision to play in the United States, and even less so by the fact that he had been talking to Nick Faldo, leading Montgomerie to suggest that Poulter already knew he was in the team as a wild card pick and that he was the only player with a "hot-line" to Faldo. It was an escalation of the hostilities that dated back to their contretemps at the Seve Trophy of 2005 and that had been simmering ever since. It had even resurfaced at the European Open at the London Club in the summer when the two had clashed over the overly noisy manner in which Montgomerie was reprimanding a cameraman.

When news of Montgomerie's comments reached Poulter in Boston, the Englishman categorically denied having received any assurances that he was already in the team, before taking the opportunity to give Montgomerie a little advice of his own. "Monty has got enough work to do this week to try to make the side," he suggested. "He should be getting his head down and trying to play good golf."

And so the transatlantic tête-à-tête continued. "It's nice," responded Montgomerie, "to be told what to do by one so young and inexperienced. The only reason we said 'a hot-line to Nick Faldo' is because Ian is the only one who has said he has been speaking to Nick. Has anyone else said that? No."

It didn't end there. Later, there would be newspaper reports of a "bust-up" between the two when they bumped into each other in a West London restaurant, a story dismissed not only by Paul Dunkley but by Poulter himself. "It literally was that Monty walked past and said, 'Congratulations for making the side and all the best in Kentucky'," he explained, a little unconvincingly. "I said, 'Thank you very much.'"

Unfairly, Poulter would bear the brunt of the criticism for his selection when, in fact, he had been nothing other than straightforward in his decisions and, for that matter, the way in which he had explained them to the golf world. Besides, it wasn't as though he had treated the decision to skip Gleneagles lightly. He had agonized long and hard about whether to play, writing down the pros and cons of both the options in front of him, just to try and make the right decision. As the highest-placed European player in the world rankings not to have made the side, and with his highest finish in a major still fresh in people's memories, it wasn't as if he didn't have a strong case for inclusion, but it was the fact that Faldo had said consistently that he wanted players who were in form on his team. "In the end it was a decision made not only for me but for my family, because we were all in the States at the time and all the travel back and forth across the Atlantic gets tiring," he told *Golf International* magazine. "I knew that Nick [Faldo] was going to have a difficult time choosing his wild cards, as there were so many good players vying for a place in his team. Darren [Clarke] was obviously playing well at the time, Paul Casey's name was in the frame, and I'm sure Nick had other names floating around in his head. That's the pressure of being captain."

Chapter 6

In that respect, then, Clarke, the undisputed hero of the Ryder Cup two years earlier at the K Club, seemed a valid choice too, having won the KLM Open in Holland the week before the announcement of the team, taken the BMW Asian Open in April and secured several top-10 finishes along the way. Certainly, Clarke wasn't blaming Poulter for his omission, however. "I think Poults has been dragged into a situation which was caused not by his own doing, but because Nick had changed his mind and gone back on it," he told Sky News. "Earlier in the year, Nick had stated he wanted his players to be in form, he wasn't going to pay particular attention to the rankings. I thought I was in good form, but unfortunately he [Faldo] changed his mind."

As it was, Montgomerie failed to make the team, either by earning an automatic place or by virtue of a captain's pick, and his Ryder Cup run, as a player at least, was at an end. Poulter, meanwhile, would also miss the cut in Boston, marking the end of his interest in the FedEx play-offs. Perhaps both men should have just got on with their golf after all. Still, Nick Faldo's team for the match against Paul Azinger's USA at Valhalla was finalized, with a mix of experienced players like Lee Westwood, Sergio Garcia and, fresh from his third major title victory at the 2008 PGA championship at Oakland Hills, Ireland's Padraig Harrington; and four rookies in the shape of England's Justin Rose and Oliver Wilson, Denmark's Soren Hansen and Northern Ireland's Graeme McDowell. And, of course, Ian Poulter, who, along with his compatriot Paul Casey, got the nod as Faldo's captain's picks.

Named after the "Hall of the Slain" in Norse mythology and set on a 486-acre plot 20 miles east of downtown Louisville, Kentucky, the Jack Nicklaus-designed Valhalla was the perfect Ryder Cup venue, featuring large undulating greens, spectacular backdrops and more than a little nod to some of Jack's favourite Scottish courses too. Though much had been done to change the course and its facilities in preparation for the Ryder Cup, including the removal of 5,000 trees to help improve viewing, no one had reckoned on the weather. On the Sunday before the Cup, as the European team headed across the Atlantic from Heathrow to Louisville, the tail end of Hurricane Ike ripped through Valhalla as it made its destructive path across the South of the US, bringing down TV towers, trees and the giant scoreboards in its wake. By the time Faldo and his team had arrived, much of Louisville was still without power.

It would take a mammoth effort by the tournament director Kenny Haigh and his team to get the site ready for the matches, but remarkably, they began on time. It would be a promising start for Faldo's Europe, too, but one not destined to last. Within an hour, they would be ahead in all of Friday morning's foursomes but soon Paul Azinger's team, inspired by some raucous home support, would eat into the lead, emerging from the session with a 3–1 advantage. Poulter, playing with his friend Justin Rose, battled valiantly but couldn't prevent Stewart Cink and Chad Campbell from winning one up at the last.

When the United States followed it up with a 2½–1½ win in the afternoon fourballs – Poulter and Rose's win over Steve Stricker and Ben Curtis being the only full point for Europe – it left the home side enjoying the largest first-day lead – three points – since the match at The Greenbrier, way back in 1979. If this was unfamiliar territory for the States, then so too was it for Europe, who had grown used to building up a lead on the first two days of play before weathering an inevitable American storm in the singles on Sunday.

But this was different and Saturday's spellbinding sessions would prove pivotal as the players upped their games and began holing putts for fun. The match would turn, as it often does, on one moment. In the third game in the afternoon fourballs, Ben Curtis and Steve Stricker seemed destined to lose against Sergio Garcia and Paul Casey, but Stricker somehow got up and down from the greenside rough at the last, his 15-foot putt securing a half point and helping to give the United States a two-point lead going into the final day.

Amid the ballyhoo, Poulter was resolute. Rising to the challenge, he seemed to be in his element and, at times, it appeared as though the US team would go to any lengths to stop him. During Saturday afternoon's fourballs, as Poulter and Graeme McDowell played Kenny Perry and Jim Furyk, Poulter was walking off the 14th tee when the American rookie Anthony Kim strode up to him and rather than walk around Poulter seemed to drop his shoulder and charge into the Woburn professional. Poulter looked perplexed. "That was awfully nice," he said.

Later, he would recall the incident and, even with the benefit of hindsight, couldn't understand just what Kim was up to, especially as he wasn't even playing in the match. "He had played in the morning and hadn't played very well and decided to walk around in the afternoon and make his point, to come to the tee-box and walk right through me, which is not what you would expect from a fellow professional," he said. "This is the Ryder Cup – it should be played in the right spirit and he should grow up. I don't know if there was a strategy there, but it didn't work. It made me more determined."

For his part, Kim still wasn't sure what had happened or why Poulter was making such an issue out of it. "I wasn't even paying attention and I looked up and Ian had just bounced off me," he said. "I didn't even see him, to be honest. I'm a lot shorter than he is, so I'm not going to throw my elbow into him. I wasn't out there to bump anybody. That's not the spirit of the Ryder Cup. This isn't football. I'm sorry he took it personally."

Come Sunday, Poulter dismantled the man whose putt had made all the difference on that crucial Saturday, Steve Stricker, beating him comfortably 3&2. But it made little difference to the result. Captain Faldo's gamble in putting his strongest players out toward the end of the singles order had backfired spectacularly and seen the likes of Poulter, McDowell, Harrington and Westwood all still out on the course by the time Jim Furyk secured the US victory with a win over Miguel Angel Jimenez. Once more, they were blown away, losing 7½–4½ in the singles to lose the match by 16½ points to 11½. After three failed attempts and for the first time in the twenty-first century, the US had won the Ryder Cup.

Faldo's team had been outplayed and the skipper himself had been out-thought and out-fought by his opposite number, Paul Azinger. The only highlight was the performance of Ian Poulter. Having played in all five sessions he had returned four points, becoming the highest points scorer in the match from either side. But for him it had been a bittersweet Ryder Cup. Though the defeat clearly hurt, he had more than justified Nick Faldo's faith in him and, of course, silenced those critics who had openly questioned his right to be in the team in the first place.

In 2010, Poulter spoke to me about that Ryder Cup. "To get picked by Nick Faldo in the first place was huge but then to back it up by being the only player to play all five sessions and emerge as the highest points scorer was just fantastic," he explained. "It's given me a lot of confidence and I like to think it really kick-started my rise up the world rankings. Obviously, I'd have rather won the Ryder Cup in 2008 but I guess you could say it was good for the future of the Ryder Cup for America to win as they'd taken two big defeats in 2004 and 2006."

As the European team left Kentucky Airport, leaving the precious Ryder Cup behind, attentions turned to the next match at Celtic Manor in 2010. Nick Faldo, soon to be knighted, would not be at that game in any official capacity, but Ian Poulter certainly would, and more than that, he had a few scores to settle.

***

It was one of those *Daily Mail* headlines that ticked almost all of the newspaper's boxes, save perhaps for the mention of benefit claimants, rising house prices and those of dubious nationality. "MONEYBAGS POULTER READY TO CASH IN AND BECOME BRITAIN'S LATEST TAX EXILE," it screamed, as though the player himself had some cunning plan to circumnavigate the demands of Her Majesty's Revenue & Customs. The truth was that Poulter's success in the United States and, to a lesser extent, around the world, had meant that he was now spending less and less time in the UK and that a full-time move to the US would benefit his bank balance massively. "Giving millions of pounds to the tax man is crazy when you're spending well below the 90 days you're permitted in Britain each year as an exile," he said. "All that money I am giving to the tax man I would much rather be giving to my kids in a few years. It is a huge sum when you're not spending any time in Britain and not making use of the facilities."

Though he made the UK sound like a leisure centre rather than his homeland, Poulter had a point. After all, not only would he no longer have to pay income tax in the UK, apart from on the prize money he won while playing back home, but he would also avoid some of the taxes that everybody else in the US were liable for because there was no state income tax payable in Florida. Put simply, it made financial sense.

Accountants, of course, tend to refer to such manoeuvres as mere "tax efficiency" but there were many more reasons for Poulter to make the move to the United States more permanent, not least the fact that his family needed a little more stability in their lives, he could get home on Sunday night and his kids would soon be entering the American education system.

Certainly, the climate in the Sunshine State appealed to the kids, especially after the endless and inevitable gloom of the UK. Now, Aimee-Leigh and Luke were outside all of the time, enjoying the new opportunities that almost-daily sunshine afforded them. Under the watchful eye of Dad, both of them would turn their hands to a little golf, although Aimee preferred her pets and her clothes, while the newest addition to the family, Lilly-Mai, just watched on oblivious to the clubs swinging all around her. Luke, though, was like his father in miniature form. Obsessed with all sports, including American football and baseball, he had also appeared to inherit the gene that made him ultra-competitive, even though he was just five years old. "He loves to win, and, fortunately, he can't stand losing," said Poulter senior. "I enjoy that, and I like the passion he shows when he loses. I see that as a huge plus. That will make him get better at whatever he wants to do."

But Poulter too had been seduced by the lifestyle in Florida, even if it meant that he couldn't now see his beloved Arsenal in action. So with his Emirates Stadium season tickets now safely in the hands of his very receptive father, Ian had decided to swap football for a new passion and treated himself to season tickets for the Orlando Magic basketball team instead. "I've become a huge basketball fan," he said in 2013. "The Orlando Magic arena is only 20 minutes from here, so we've got a suite there and go to every game we can with family and friends."

After five years of criss-crossing the Atlantic, the move to the United States had not only brought some much-needed constancy but was a clear indication of Poulter's drive and desire to try and cement his place in golf's elite. And it suited him too. Now he could finish a tournament on a Sunday and be home that evening. Sometimes the family would be there to join him too. Things, it seemed, were working out just fine.

Now, Poulter seemed determined to address everything that stood in his way; he even got his eyes sorted, finally. For nine years, Ian's eyes had been causing him problems, not that you would have really noticed watching him play the game. Short-sighted, with a -1.5 prescription, Poulter also had a stigmatism that he had never had corrected, the net result being that he had to wear contact lenses, a solution which often made his eyes sore and made reading his putts difficult, especially when the light was fading.

In 2003, Poulter sought advice from a Harley Street specialist in London but had been advised that the risks of surgery were too great to warrant an operation. Six years on, though, and the technology had advanced sufficiently for him to seek a second opinion from a specialist in Florida and, assured that the procedure was now safe, he had gone ahead and had the lasik surgery on both eyes. Within six hours, both of his eyes were almost perfect again.

By the following day, it was as if someone had transplanted them for a pair of 20:20s.

If the eye surgery had proved to be a revelation, so too would be another new discovery in Poulter's life. Now, other than the start of the 21st NATO Summit in Strasbourg, France, the date of Wednesday, April 3, 2009 was largely unremarkable but in the rollercoaster existence of Ian James Poulter it would prove to be a pivotal one, not because he won a major or landed another big title but because it was the day that he was "born" on the social networking site Twitter. Under the username @IanJamesPoulter, he had suddenly found a platform that suited him perfectly, a new medium where he could keep his fans updated with everything that was happening in his life, from major breaking news to, more often than not, the less significant occurrences too. There was no longer any need for a press conference or for Paul Dunkley to issue a statement. Now, he could just grab his BlackBerry and, in the space of 140 carefully or perhaps casually chosen characters, could tell the world just how he was feeling after a particular round, what his thoughts were ahead of a tournament or even what he had just had for breakfast.

For those in the public eye, of course, Twitter is little more than an online popularity contest and a chance to prove just how much better regarded you are than your contemporaries, even if it is in a flimsy and ethereal virtual world. But evidence of just how popular Poulter and, perhaps, his approach to the game were becoming was clear as soon as he unleashed himself on Twitter. Within a couple of weeks, for example, he already had 200,000 followers, around half of the total of the then leader in golf's Twitterati, the American Stewart Cink. "Some people don't like it but it's a good thing, surely?" he told Donald McRae in the *Guardian* soon after he took to the social network. "If you're sitting in an office, doing nine to five, this is a great insight into pro golf. Where else are you going to see the inside of a players' lounge at a major? Lots of people can't afford to go to major tournaments, so I try and give them a little extra."

Certainly, Ian had found a new obsession in Twitter and once he had started there was no stopping him. At the rain-affected US Open at Bethpage, where he would finish in a creditable tie for 18th, he tweeted that he "had sushi last night. Thought it was apt. Going to feel like a fish out there today." Yes, from the mundane to the momentous, the sensational to the surreal, Poulter's new rapid-fire updates had found a keen and receptive constituency, and one who couldn't care less if his spelling was of a standard that would have infuriated his teachers back at Barclay. "I'm getting the piss taken because of my spelling," he admitted, "but I didn't grow up chewing on a Collins dictionary. It's something you do on the BlackBerry when you've got a spare second – and you fire it off. C'mon, the banter is more important than the spelling."

Banter. It's an awful word, much overused in the world of sport. It's a word that's often used to excuse the inexcusable and actually explains very little. Still, in Poulter's case it seemed to be the perfect description for his regular Twitter musings. But then, increasingly, he had a lot to talk about. At The Players Championship at the TPC at Sawgrass – the game's unofficial fifth major – Poulter's sensational short game carried him through to a well-deserved second place behind the runaway winner, Sweden's Henrik Stenson. It was a solid and impressive display that, but for a 75 in the difficult conditions of Saturday's third round, could have been even better. But he wasn't too disappointed. Yes, he had missed out on taking one of the game's much-coveted titles but the small matter of a cheque for $1,026,000 went a long way toward making up for the absence of another trophy in the cabinet.

What was interesting about Poulter's performance in The Players Championship was that it not only served to show how comfortable he now felt in his adopted homeland but also how natural it felt for him to be rubbing shoulders with those in the higher echelons of the PGA Tour pecking order. But it also showed how Poulter was using his greatest asset – his self-belief – in helping him adapt to Tour golf in the States. "I've learned to try and use confidence in a slightly different way and to never give up," he told the media after his final round. "It [used to be] all or nothing, where now I think I'm a more consistent player and I understand myself a bit more and I understand when to attack and when to kind of back off."

The size of Poulter's prize at the end of The Players Championship also appeared to validate his decision to move over to the USA full-time. While the Players was one of the biggest tournaments in golf (with the biggest purse on the PGA Tour), the contrast with the event happening across the pond on the European Tour could not have been more pronounced. There, at the BMW Italian Open, a three-way tie for second spot between France's Raphael Jacquelin, Wales' Robert Rock and the larger-than-life, all-American hero John Daly – a two-time major winner, lest we forget – netted each man just €96,940. While that, obviously, was still a significant return for those golfers (and in everyday terms it was three times the average salary in the UK), it was nevertheless dwarfed by the sums on offer on the PGA Tour.

Indeed, in his first eight events of the 2009 PGA Tour season, Poulter was now averaging nearly $220,000 per event, an amount you wouldn't get for winning most of the European Tour tournaments. And this despite not lifting a trophy in any of them and only recording three top-10 finishes. But then everyone seemed to be better off playing on the PGA Tour. In 2008, for example, the top 104 players on the end-of-year money list all earned over $1 million in prize money alone. In Europe, only the top 15 players earned over €1 million, which, even allowing for the exchange rate, shows just how far adrift the European Tour lagged in terms of financial reward.

Over the years, the decision to move to the US has proved vexatious for many European players. Some, like the six-time major winner Nick Faldo, have had little problem with committing to playing on the PGA Tour full-time. Indeed, Faldo did it twice, first in 1981 for six years before rejoining it in 1995, a year before he won his last major at the Masters. Others, like Colin Montgomerie, however, remained resolutely committed to the European Tour, preferring to be bigger fishes in what was, undeniably, a much smaller pond. Montgomerie's decision, especially, was intriguing and not just because he had enjoyed unprecedented and record-breaking success on the European Tour, eventually winning a total of eight Order of Merit titles. It seemed to be at odds with other players because he, like so many of today's top European professionals, had been through the US collegiate system, playing for the golf team at Houston Baptist University before turning professional in 1987. But the Scot had decided to concentrate on playing golf on his home Tour instead, leading to accusations that he was simply coasting in his career and not testing himself against the world's best. "I don't know what he wants," said Nick Faldo, for example. "I'm surprised he hasn't done something different as a challenge. But he likes to earn his fat cheques each week, and there's no harm in that – if you're motivated by that. A few are. Most of us go for 10 claret jugs. He's in a comfort zone, and I think he just enjoys it. He goes out and wins a couple of hundred thousand each week and goes home. I'd be comfortable if I did that every week."

In that respect, Poulter differed from many of his contemporaries, including Ryder Cup team-mates like Graeme McDowell, Paul Casey and Luke Donald, all of whom had left college and all but walked straight into the well-paid ranks of professional golf. That's not to say they didn't deserve it – their talent made them clear and obvious prospects for the professional game – but none of them really knew what it was like to struggle or to wonder how the bills were going to be paid. And while Montgomerie had doubtless consumed a few Mars Bars in his time, it's unlikely he ever had occasion to serve them to a 24-handicapper with a bad attitude and a hand-me-down half set.

Perhaps that's one of the reasons why Montgomerie and Poulter don't exactly see eye to eye. After all, they are complete and polar opposites, with little in common other than they happen to have the same occupation, a fact that was certainly exposed during the Seve Trophy of 2009. This, lest we forget, was the competition where the two men had had their first major difference of opinion four years earlier and now it would happen again.

The Seve Trophy (by now called the "Vivendi Seve Trophy" following a sponsorship deal with the French media giant) had become known, rightly or wrongly, as one of the tournaments that those players with designs on playing in the Ryder Cup could use to help put them in the spotlight. The 2009 edition of the event – the sixth time it had been played – pitted Paul McGinley's Great Britain and Ireland against Thomas Bjorn's Continental Europe and while both skippers harboured thoughts of one day captaining Europe in the Ryder Cup itself, the event in Paris would be overshadowed by yet another unseemly dispute between the man appointed as captain of the European side for the 2010 matches, Colin Montgomerie, and the player who had decided not to participate in the event, Ian Poulter.

Though Montgomerie had no part to play in the event – he was only there to keep tabs on some of the players who might feature in his team for Celtic Manor – he nevertheless chose the occasion to question the commitment not of all the players who had failed to show, but to single out Ian Poulter instead. So while the likes of Justin Rose, Sergio Garcia and Luke Donald all opted out to concentrate on the Tour Championship in Atlanta, Montgomerie publicly called into question Poulter's commitment. "I just feel that when you are selected for your country more of an effort might well have been made. Ian Poulter, not having qualified for the Tour Championship and having been picked for the last Ryder Cup team, I felt that a little more effort might have been made to come here."

What made Montgomerie's outburst all the more vindictive was that he had also insisted that he "didn't want to make a big issue of this", even though no other players were singled out for not making the trip. Indeed, he was so determined not to make a big deal out of it that he carried on piling into Poulter when he was interviewed for Radio Five Live soon after, arguing that the fact that he had enjoyed a captain's pick for the Ryder Cup at Valhalla a year earlier meant he should have made more of an effort. "I just feel that, having been picked as a wild card last time, Ian Poulter could have given back a little bit more than he has this week," he grumbled.

For once, Poulter's response was remarkably restrained. "It would have been great to play the Vivendi Trophy, but it's very difficult to play every event," he explained via his new mouthpiece, Twitter. "It's important not to burn out. I really want to be fresh and strong for the Ryder Cup qualifying events," adding, "The Ryder Cup means everything to me."

He even had some kind words for his nemesis, although they could have been construed as those of a man with one eye on a wild card place in the Ryder Cup team. "I think Monty will make a great captain, with such an impressive Ryder Cup record he knows what it takes," he said, without the merest suggestion of sarcasm. "He will inspire."

The question, of course, was whether he would inspire Poulter and, more pertinently, whether he would actually select him should the Englishman fail to qualify for the 2010 Ryder Cup team – Montgomerie's team – as of right.

For Poulter, though, the running feud with Montgomerie, a player at the tail end of his career but who, crucially, held most of the cards when it came to Poulter's Ryder Cup dreams was but a sideshow in a year and career that was progressing nicely. Clearly, his appearance, demeanour and attitude irritated the ultra-conservative Scot, but maybe it was something more. Maybe there was a part of Montgomerie that saw in Poulter the kind of get up and go that he himself lacked, the very same traits that had perhaps prevented him from getting up and going to the United States and the PGA Tour himself.

No matter how bad, or even tiresome, the relationship with Montgomerie got, it couldn't take anything away from what had been a stellar year for Poulter. The decision to move to the United States had proved more successful than he could have imagined in taking 25th place on the final end-of-season PGA Tour Money List, ahead of the likes of Luke Donald and Ernie Els, with $2,431,001 in prize money safely banked. But his success in America, especially in those events co-sanctioned by the European Tour, had also seen him enjoy a lofty placing on the European Tour's new Race to Dubai list, a competition launched in response to the PGA Tour's FedEx Cup and in a bid to curtail the exodus of talent across the Atlantic. Finishing ninth, Poulter guaranteed himself a share of a $7.5 million bonus as one of the top-15 placed players on the European Tour.

Nobody, not even Colin Montgomerie, could really deny him his success.

Chapter 7
Grand Designs

@IanJamesPoulter
@PaulAzinger Zinger I will yell come on, on every putt that is holed, my bum will be in the air all day picking them out the hole.
In response to the 2008 Ryder Cup captain Paul Azinger's dislike of Poulter's overly vociferous celebration of putts

When Ian Poulter made his now infamous comments about it being "just me and Tiger" back in 2008 he, like most other people in the game, had quite reasonably assumed that Woods, in all likelihood, would remain the pre-eminent force in professional golf for some time to come. He was, after all, closing in on Jack Nicklaus' record of 18 major titles and well on the way to becoming sport's first ever billionaire.

But on Friday, November 27, 2009, Woods' life imploded. Leaving his house at 02.25 hours, the world number one had crashed his Cadillac Escalade into a fire hydrant at the end of his drive. Initial news reports suggested Woods had been seriously injured in the crash, although facial lacerations were all he would need treatment for. While the accident itself was big news, what then unfolded was unlike any other sports – or celebrity – scandal in living memory and in the days and weeks that followed, the career of arguably the greatest golfer in the history of the game imploded in a whirlwind of sleazy tabloid revelations.

Every day, it seemed as though another woman would step forward as more lurid and lascivious tales of Woods' indiscretions emerged. Cocktail waitresses, porn stars, models and mums, there seemed to be no shortage of ex-lovers only too eager to come forward to tell their tales of their times with the Tiger. Within days, his wife Elin Nordegren would move out, taking their kids, Sam and Charlie, with her.

As the coverage intensified, Woods had headed to Mississippi and to the Pine Grove sex addiction centre in Hattiesburg in a bid to save his marriage, his career and, no doubt, his sanity. His sponsors soon got spooked too, as Gatorade, AT&T, Accenture and GM Motors would all announce they were parting ways with the fallen star and Woods would be forced into an extraordinary media statement-cum-apology broadcast live across the world's TV networks in which he explained that he had felt "entitled" to act in the manner that he did. He also announced an indefinite break from the professional game before heading off back to Pine Grove for further treatment.

Woods' demise was as spectacular and shocking as it had been rapid. Here was a player, a man who had built his career not just on a God-given golf game but on an image that was cleaner than clean. The family man. The doting dad. The good guy. And here he was, the greatest sportsman of his generation imploding in a blizzard of sleaze.

Like everybody else in the watching world, Poulter was transfixed by what had happened down the road in Isleworth. While the story of a golfer's extra-marital affair may not have been worthy of that many column inches the fact that it was the most recognizable sportsman in the world on one hand combined with the sheer and almost incomprehensible scale of the philandering on the other made for an irresistible news story, guaranteed to run and run. Like many other golfers who were quizzed on the hottest of all topics, Poulter would be at pains to distance himself from the scandal and concentrate instead on Woods' record in the game. "It's his private life, and I don't know him away from the golf course," he told *Golf Digest's* Rich Lerner. "The only Tiger I know is No. 1 in the world, the most ruthless person I've ever seen, the most focused person I've ever seen. I don't understand how you hole 30-foot putts time and again. It's freaky. Defies all logic."

The scandal had taken everyone by surprise, although the idea that nobody in the game knew anything about Woods' behaviour, including his caddie Steve Williams and his long-time agent Mark Steinberg, seemed remarkable. Certainly, people were talking about little else at the Omega Mission Hills World Cup in China, where news of Tiger's troubles had reached the players.

"Probably disbelief more than anything as to what had happened," said the Irishman Graeme McDowell. "There was plenty of Tiger Woods questions going on. Yeah, I think everyone was pretty worked up about it, it was big news."

The following week a select band of players were back in the United States to play in Woods' own tournament, the Chevron World Challenge at Sherwood Country Club at Thousand Oaks in California. While it wasn't an official PGA Tour event as such, the event, in aid of the Tiger Woods Foundation, still offered world ranking points and a prize fund in excess of $5 million which, given there were only 18 players in the field, meant a nice pay-day for the happy few who managed to tee it up.

Woods, of course, wouldn't make it to his own party – ticket holders were offered full refunds – and while his absence would be blamed on the injuries he sustained in the car crash, it was clear to anybody who had switched on a TV set in the past week that they were really the least of his concerns. Woods' place in the field would be taken by McDowell who, grateful for what was a very lucrative and unexpected opportunity, spoke further about the fall-out from the story. "Not having him here is obviously a huge disappointment," he said. "It's a huge disappointment for golf in general, really. I mean [Woods] is everything that's good about our sport. He's an iconic image in our sport."

It was a strange line to take, especially the bit about Woods being "everything that's good about our sport", but then one should never be rude about one's host, even if they're otherwise detained. For Poulter, though, an invite to the Chevron World Challenge felt like he had finally found his true place in the world of professional golf. But then he had deserved it. On the PGA Tour in 2009 he had made 13 of 17 cuts, five of which were top-10 finishes, while over in Europe, he made 10 of 11 cuts, finishing in the top 10 on three occasions. It had been a good year, a very good year.

Poulter, resplendent in pink and purple tartan trousers, would begin in scintillating form and his first-round 68 could have been even better, had it not been for a wayward drive and a double bogey at the final hole. Still, a share of the lead with the 2007 Masters champion Zach Johnson would be welcome, not least because it was the first time he had ever held the lead after 18 holes on American soil.

While Poulter's challenge would falter, perhaps inevitably given that this was his sixth straight week of competition, his week would still be a success as a tie for fifth place and another cheque, this time for a few dollars short of a quarter of a million, however, would be safely banked. Jim Furyk, the man with the swing sent straight from hell, bagged a pair of 67s to take the title and the first prize of $1.35 million.

From mid-December, Poulter decided to take a month off from playing. He needed it. While holding down places on both the PGA Tour and the European Tour certainly gave him options when it came to his schedules this inevitably made his life more hectic and 28 official events played over the course of the year, plus a couple of silly season events thrown in for good measure at the end of the year, meant plenty of money in the bank but less time for the really important things in life, like his family.

The break worked wonders. Refreshed and reinvigorated, he bagged a second-place finish at the Abu Dhabi Golf Championship on his now annual jaunt to the Middle East and, a month later, he won the WGC-Accenture Match Play Championship at The Gallery Golf Club in Tucson, Arizona – his first win in the United States.

Even by his own admission, Poulter was playing the best golf of his career. His short game, so long the bedrock of his better rounds, was strong and solid, while 27 birdies in the five matches leading up to the final against Paul Casey suggested that his form with the short stick was none too shabby either, as he beat Justin Leonard, Adam Scott, Jeev Milkha Singh, Thongchai Jaidee and Sergio Garcia. In the 36-hole final, meanwhile, he had plundered 11 birdies en route to a 4&2 victory.

As well as claiming the biggest cheque of his career – an eye-watering $1.4 million – Poulter also rose six places in the world rankings to number five, the highest of his career. Other accolades would follow, including being named The European Tour Race To

Dubai Golfer of the Month for February and claiming the Shot of the Month trophy too, awarded for a greenside chip that he very nearly holed for an eagle at the 15th hole in the match against Casey.

But in the days that followed his breakthrough victory one thing was patently clear. People had suddenly stopped talking about Poulter's clothes or his hairstyle or his car collection. Instead they were finally talking about his golf, which, at times, had been nothing short of phenomenal. Indeed, in winning the event, he had been so dominant that he had only had to play 114 holes all week; only Tiger Woods, with 112 holes in 2003, had played fewer holes in the course of victory. "I've had an interesting ride from a lot of people's point of view of how I present myself on the golf course, as opposed to how well I can actually perform," Poulter said. "This to me is very pleasing to be able to be in that position now. I guess [number] five in the world stands for more than just what I wear on the golf course."

In a game still rocking from the Tiger Woods scandal, Poulter's emergence as one of the new great hopes for the sport had come at the ideal time. Now 34 and at his peak in golfing terms, he was still concerned with how he looked on the golf course – he had a fashion range to think off, after all – but the focus and determination he now had was clear for all to see. Interestingly, Poulter was achieving success in a game where his relative lack of length off the tee put him at a distinct disadvantage. Where once golf courses were "Tiger-proofed" now there was a new breed of boomers, like Dustin Johnson and Bubba Watson, who were, on average, 20 to 30 yards longer than Poulter (who averaged 286.8 yards off the tee in 2010). It was a difference that merely served to reinforce just how impressive his touch in and around the green was. "I probably put 30 per cent of my practice into my short game," he told me in 2011, "and every professional works hard at their short game: Mickelson, Tiger, Harrington – they've all got amazing short games and it's no coincidence that those are the guys that are always in there, come the end of a tournament."

Poulter's good form would carry through most of the spring and even when things didn't quite go to plan, for example at the Transitions Championship at Palm Harbor, Florida in mid-March, where he surprisingly missed the cut, he didn't let it worry him. Indeed, it is typical of his approach to the game that he is able to divorce himself from a bad round or the occasional setback. There is no great post-mortem or investigation into what went wrong or why. To his credit, Poulter just parks the problems and manages to move on. "I don't even watch the highlights of the events I've played in," he told me in an interview for *Sky Sports* magazine in 2010. "The last thing I want to do after playing five hours of golf is sit down and watch some more. I want to do something else – I'm not a golf nerd."

You could tell just how happy Poulter was with his game by the way he came to life in the Tavistock Cup, the annual knockabout played between the two neighbouring Orlando estates of Lake Nona and Isleworth. In his and Henrik Stenson's game against Robert Allenby and JB Holmes, for example, he made five birdies on the back nine to seal the overall win for his Lake Nona team, 17–13.

By the time the Masters came around in April, Poulter was feeling confident and composed, and all the signs suggested he was about to mount a serious tilt at his first major. At the WGC-CA Championships at Doral two weeks prior he had produced what he would describe as one of the "best ten rounds of my career" when he finished with a sensational 64 around the famed Blue Monster course and while the placing itself wasn't spectacular – he ended in a tie for 37th – he couldn't have been happier with his form. "Obviously if people think I've got a better chance (at Augusta) than I've ever had in the past, then that's great," he said. "I'm going to have as much confidence as I've ever had in the past going into that week so there's no reason not to ride that all the way."

As the first major of the year, there was always a sense of anticipation and expectation ahead of the Masters but this year the ante had been upped by the return of Tiger Woods to competitive golf. After a four-month self-imposed exile, Woods had decided to use Augusta, where he already had four wins to his name, as the setting for his return and while his life had been torn apart off the golf course, it was business as usual for him on it. He still had Steve Williams, his caddie; he still had Hank Haney, his coach; and he still had Mark "Steiny" Steinberg, his agent. The only people who would not be there with him were Elin and his two children.

Even the Augusta National Golf Club chairman, Billy Payne, was heralding Tiger's return as something akin to a second coming. "We at Augusta hope and pray our great champion will begin his new life here tomorrow in a positive, hopeful and constructive manner," he said, skipping over all the stuff about serial adultery. "This year, it will not be just for him, but for all of us who believe in second chances."

This would be Poulter's sixth chance at the Masters and while he had made the cut in each of his previous visits, he had never really troubled the engravers, a tie for 13th in 2007 being his best finish. While the frisson around Augusta was palpable, he seemed more relaxed than ever. Having hired a house on Magnolia Lane for the week, he had brought the entire Poulter family with him and at the traditional par-three tournament had even got his children, Luke and Aimee-Leigh, to caddie for him, ruffling Luke's hair as the boy drained a 20-footer in front of a stunned crowd.

What made Poulter's appearance all the more fascinating was that not only had he taken a two-week break from the Tour ahead of the Masters, visiting the course to plot and plan his way around, but his grouping, with the USA's Steve Stricker and Japan's Yuta Ikeda, would be going out directly in front of Tiger Woods and his group. Inevitably, this would mean much bigger crowds as people took their places early to get a glimpse of their fallen hero back in action, but for Poulter it couldn't have worked out better. Playing to the crowds, he opened with an impressive four-under-par 68, and then repeated the trick in the second round to leave himself and his co-leader, Lee Westwood, two shots clear of a chasing pack that included Phil Mickelson and, ominously, Tiger Woods.

After 36 holes, Ian Poulter, the former assistant professional/confectionery salesman, was leading the Masters and he celebrated as any boy from Hertfordshire would. "Just sat down for my dinner, steak and ale pie, couple of spuds, get in there," he tweeted.

Those were giddy times indeed and on the Saturday, he made his move. The only trouble was it was in the wrong direction. Playing with Westwood, he finished the outward nine in level-par, with back-to-back bogeys followed by gutsy back-to-back birdies, but made a bogey on the 11th and a double bogey on the famous par-three 12th after finding himself plugged in the bunker. The net result was a two-over-par round of 74 that sent him spiralling back down the leaderboard, just as the rest of the field seemed to be heading the other way. An untidy 73 in the final round, meanwhile, would see his challenge finally wither.

It would prove to be a wholly frustrating weekend for Poulter and one that was the polar opposite of the promising first two days. Not only had one of his first real chances of landing a major evaporated but all the lessons he had learned in researching the course beforehand had been rendered useless by some uncharacteristically sub-standard positional play off the tee. Even the four horses he had backed in the Grand National back home had failed to deliver.

For most players, a tie for 10th at the Masters would be a cause for some celebration, not least because it guarantees you a place in the field for the following year's competition. But for Poulter it was beyond disappointing. "That really shouldn't have happened," he reflected. "I drove it very poorly on the Saturday, which took me back a few shots and out of position. I played better on Sunday but just couldn't manage to hole the putts. You then have to chase it and be aggressive. You can do that at Augusta but it's a classic risk-and-reward golf course. All it takes is one or two bad shots and you can come unstuck."

The tournament would be won by Phil Mickelson – his third Green Jacket. It was a flawless, bogey-free final round of golf by the Californian and as he pulled away from Westwood over the back nine he emphasized his superiority with one of the finest shots ever seen, not merely at the Masters but in recent history. Stuck in the trees on the high side of 13th hole and with a gap barely big enough to squeeze through ahead of him, the left-hander ripped a six-iron toward the green and as his ball cleared the stream guarding the putting surface it landed softly, coming to rest just a few feet from the hole. It was the shot of a true champion.

The much-heralded return of Tiger Woods, meanwhile, would end neither in humiliation as many had predicted – nothing could embarrass him any more – nor victorious redemption. Yes, there were flashes of his genius and yes, there was the same irate scowl whenever the ball failed to do as it was told, but without any competitive experience and playing off memory, he had still exceeded most people's expectations in finishing in a tie for fourth.

Whatever you thought of Woods the man, his mere presence at the Masters had shown just how central a figure that Woods the player had become in professional golf. It's often said that no one individual is bigger than their chosen sport, but in the case of Woods, a player whose appearance in a tournament guarantees everything from bigger galleries and viewing figures to increased advertising revenue and larger purses, it seemed hard to argue otherwise.

For Poulter, Woods was still the player against whom all others would be measured. "It's great to have Tiger back," he told me in 2010. "At the Masters he hit some great shots and some poor shots but, you know, he hadn't played for months, he didn't play anywhere near as well as he can, and he still finished fourth. That's ominous. Everybody in the game owes him a lot for what he's done for the game of golf in the last 12 years. He's a truly great player and he'll be back to winning ways very soon."

While Woods was battling to hold on to everything from his sponsors to his sanity, Poulter too was finding himself in hot water, only not for any of the reasons that had seen Woods so publicly humiliated. Soon after the Masters, he had settled down to watch the midweek derby match between his beloved Arsenal and Tottenham. It would not be a good night for the Gunners as Spurs ran out 2–1 winners – their first league win over Arsenal since November 1999 – a victory that all but ended any lingering chance Arsène Wenger's side had of winning the Premier League title that season.

Poulter, to coin a familiar football phrase, was gutted. "Not talking about football after being beat by the yids," he tweeted. Though it was meant to be a disgruntled post from a football fan, it was one that immediately drew widespread criticism for its perceived anti-Semitic stance. Spurs, after all, was a club that was known for its substantial Jewish fan base and, indeed, many of its fans had adopted the moniker in a self-deprecating way to reclaim the word. But for Poulter to use it, and in such a public way, provoked strong and immediate reaction. "He should know better," said a Tottenham Hotspur Supporters' Trust spokeswoman, before adding, "but we've never known an Arsenal fan to be gracious in defeat." Sensing a public relations disaster, Poulter removed the offending Tweet before issuing an unreserved apology. "Didn't mean to offend anybody with my football Tweet last night," he said. "Very sorry if I did. I am not racial in any way."

Racial or racist, it didn't matter. He hadn't really meant to offend anyone with his blokey football banter but had inadvertently been caught out by his post-match ire and his itchy Twitter fingers. Even during the World Cup in South Africa in the summer, Poulter was getting busy online again, winding up American fans ahead of England's opening group game against the US. "You guys havent got a chance against england, its like england vs usa in basketball, sorry but its the truth," he said, before the argument escalated into the relative merits of mainstream American sports: "how can you call it kickball, football you use your feet, what game do you call football, throw catch girls in big padsball." He may have been supremely confident about Fabio Capello's England team, but he shouldn't have been. The match would end in a disappointing 1–1 stalemate.

What is remarkable is that someone as busy as Poulter, with all his many commitments, can find the time not just to post the odd Tweet but often to engage in long and involved exchanges on Twitter. You might assume that after a day on the golf course and a few hours on the practice range, he might just want to kick back and relax, maybe catch up on some TV or read a book. But not so. For a start he has only ever admitted to reading one book – Thomas Hauser's excellent biography of Muhammad Ali – and besides, there's just too much fun to be had at his fingertips. After all, who else could resist putting photos of top golfers like Tiger Woods, Phil Mickelson, Rory McIlroy and Bubba Watson through an app called "Fat Booth" and then posting their newly-plump visages straight to them?

But is he just adept at spreading his brand with all the modern means at his disposal, or is it something more sinister? Is Poulter actually a Twitter-holic? It's quite possible. In 2012, a survey by the University of Chicago found that using social media can be more addictive than cigarettes and alcohol in that such sites can trigger a burst of the addictive neurotransmitter dopamine, while the status and numbers of followers of fellow users can also provoke feelings of jealousy and anxiety. Not that Poulter would agree. "Sometimes how I explain myself to the media can come across in a slightly different way to how I would mean to say things," he told the *Guardian*. "I get pissed off if I feel someone hasn't written the story in the way that I tried to explain because people's and fans' opinions of me get swayed one way or another by what they read in the papers. With Twitter I am in control of whatever it is I want to say."

Which is true, of course, even if it is something that crosses the line. When Rory McIlroy blew a gilt-edged chance to win his first major at the Masters in 2011, Poulter consoled him by posting a picture of a road sign for the town "Choker". "I was a bit worried when I saw other people's reaction but Rory and I have been exchanging banter for years and we often push it to the limit," he explained later. "The first time I saw him after Augusta I asked if I'd caused any offence and he just said no – we both give each other plenty of stick."

One journalist who has seen Poulter grow from part-golfer, part-clothes horse into one of the world's best players is Lawrence Donegan, former golf correspondent for the *Guardian* newspaper. "I've been around professional athletes for 15 years and I can say without hesitation that Poulter is unique in his inability to hide what he really thinks. I hasten to add this is a compliment, not a complaint. He is a journalist's dream – not afraid to say what he thinks, not afraid to give the PC-police a heart attack, but daring to utter what others in his line of work would never dare.

"Likewise, he is a Twitter user's dream. Sure, some of the stuff he tweets won't be to everyone's taste – some of it isn't to my taste, and I like the guy! – but if you want to know what Poulter is really like it is all there for the general public, captured forever in 140-character vignettes. Is it a bad idea that he's on Twitter? Don't be daft. What do we want from our sporting heroes – blandness or bluntness; some PR man's vision of what a working-class golfer made good should be like or the reality that is @IanJamesPoulter? It's no contest in my eyes."

***

Living in Orlando, and in the United States more generally, suited Ian Poulter, and not just because Americans tended to embrace rather than frown upon his obsession for big, gas-guzzling cars. In the hermetically-sealed world of the Lake Nona estate, moreover, he had found a home from home, where all the street names harked back to England – he lived on Covent Garden Drive, for example – and where he could still lay his hands on the really important things in life: the bacon sandwiches, the PG Tips, the occasional takeaway curry. Yes, you could take the boy out of Hertfordshire but, it seemed, you couldn't take Hertfordshire out of the boy. "I feel just like an Englishman living in America," he said.

That's not to say he wasn't welcomed in the United States. Far from it. If anything, Poulter's profile was now at a level where his performances on the golf course and his attitude off it were attracting not simply newspaper headlines but lucrative sponsorship deals too, with the likes of MasterCard, Mutual of Omaha and Marquis Jet all happy to pay the Englishman for the privilege of a logo on his shirt, which, by now, was fast becoming not unlike the overalls of a Formula One driver.

Indeed, Poulter's burgeoning profile was now such that he was even being called to appear on chat shows, turning up in a leather jacket on NBC's *Late Night with Jimmy Fallon*, for example, to play the host at the latest instalment of EA Sports' (another of Ian's sponsors) successful golf computer game, *Tiger Woods' PGA TOUR*. Maybe that's what Poulter meant when he said it would be just him and Tiger.

Still, the fact that Poulter was now being thought of as guest material on prime-time television – even though he wasn't a major winner – was the clearest indication yet that his desire to break the mould of what most people perceived as the archetypal golfer was paying real dividends, both professionally and financially. "Living there [in the United States], my profile has definitely changed," he explained ahead of the Open Championship at St Andrews in 2010.

"I'm being used in advertising much more, and it's refreshing to be recognized as one of the top players. It's hard being torn in two different directions, between the sport and business, but I love the fun side of this game."

Of course, there were more tangible signs that life was good for Poulter, other than wearing expensive leather jackets and playing computer games on network chat shows, of course. For one, there was the new holiday home he was having built in the Bahamas, a five-bedroom palace of a pad that sat on the beach in a gated community, with access to a water park, marina, sports and equestrian centres and, as luck would have it, a golf course too. It was, as Poulter himself described it, "quite an awesome place."

Even the way he was now getting to his events was decidedly more upmarket. Where once he might have cadged a lift on another player's plane, now he used Marquis Jets (a subsidiary of NetJets) to get around. He didn't own a jet (yet) but he could book out blocks of time on one so he could get home that bit quicker. Sometimes it made perfect sense. On other occasions, however, it seemed a little frivolous. Once, for example, it was reported that he had taken a five-minute flight on a Gulfstream G4 to get home from a shoot for a commercial, a fact that would have gone unnoticed had he not decided to tweet about it. "Be home in 5 mins I will post take off and landing when I'm on wireless loads of footage," he wrote.

At which point, of course, he found himself on the receiving end of some stinging criticism from readers who were questioning the carbon footprint of taking such a short journey. "Tree huggers stop it your [sic] boring me, I guess i should have set off 5 days ago and gone on my push bike."

But Poulter would find some strident support from within the game, which was unusual, not least because golfers never really choose to air their personal political views in such a prominent and public manner. "AL GORE," tweeted the victorious 2008 Ryder Cup captain Paul Azinger, leaping to the Englishman's defence, "the ultimate hypocritical tree hugger set the standard high for private air travel. Friendly skies to you Ian."

It was a sign of Poulter's growing reputation in America that he could now rely on some of the PGA Tour's senior statesmen to come to his aid, not that he really needed it, and that feeling of acceptance, the sense that he had finally found his true place in the professional game, appeared to be working wonders for his game. His impressive form over the qualification period, especially in 2010, had already cemented his place in the European Ryder Cup team for Celtic Manor.

In retrospect, it was fortunate that he had played his way into the side as come decision day, the team captain, Colin Montgomerie, was forced to choose two players from four who all had a genuine claim to a place in the team. As it was, Montgomerie would pick Luke Donald and the three-time major champion Padraig Harrington as his captain's picks, leaving Paul Casey, who had appeared in the last three Ryder Cups, and Justin Rose, who had won twice on the PGA Tour in 2010, on the sidelines. It's interesting to think what might have happened had Poulter been one of those four players. Would Montgomerie have picked him, given everything that had gone on before? It was a moot point, obviously, but you suspect that maybe Poulter would not have had the good fortune he enjoyed at Valhalla in 2008.

But as the Ryder Cup approached, it was imperative that all members of the European team were pulling in the same direction, singing from the same hymn sheet… or any other cliché that golf commentators seemed to be rolling out *ad nauseum*. For the most part, this wasn't an issue. Even though life on Tour could occasionally be a lonely and isolated existence for the players, the Europeans never seemed to have much of a problem hunting in a pack every two years. Virtually the only potential problem that arose, then, was the often volatile relationship between captain Colin Montgomerie and the man who was fast taking over Montgomerie's old role as the on-course leader of the team, Ian Poulter.

For years the two men had been spending an inordinate amount of time taking pot shots at each other at regular intervals, when really they should have just chosen to forget about it and save some newsprint, or, in Poulter's case, some characters. As it was, though, the two had played out a series of unedifying spats, with neither of them seemingly prepared to back down. But for the Ryder Cup – Monty's Ryder Cup – a truce had been called and their many differences had, for the sake of team unity, been resolved or at least buried for the time being. "Thankfully it's all in the past now," insisted Montgomerie, just days ahead of the match in Wales. "I've got the utmost respect for him for the way he is getting everything out of his game and he respects the position I am in as captain. It's never easy being a pick at the Ryder Cup but look at the way he totally vindicated Nick Faldo's decision to give him a wild card last time. Now he's in the team on merit and I'm very happy about that."

For his part, Poulter was also talking up their special relationship and making light of the many clashes they had experienced across recent years. "I think the chemistry is absolutely great," he said. "We understand each other very well. I'm a passionate player and so is Colin. That's potentially why we might have had the odd clash. But as I said, we understand each other. I respect him, he respects me – I think it's worked out great."

After the defeat in 2008 – Europe's first reverse in the Ryder Cup since the infamous and ill-tempered encounter at Brookline in 1999 – Montgomerie had become obsessed with returning the trophy to European hands. The match at Valhalla had been the first Ryder Cup he had missed as a player after a run of eight matches stretching back to his debut at the "War On The Shore" at Kiawah Island in 1991. Now, as captain, he was intent on adding the crowning glory to his remarkable Ryder Cup career by wresting the cup away from Corey Pavin's USA team.

Articulate, authoritative and with an almost peerless record in the Ryder Cup, Montgomerie certainly ticked all the boxes when it came to his captaincy, and though he was clearly past his prime as a player the fact he was still plying his trade on the European Tour meant he had a sound appreciation of which players were on form and which ones were perhaps struggling with their games.

As skipper, Montgomerie would leave nothing to chance in his bid to reclaim the Ryder Cup. All of his four vice-captains – Thomas Bjorn, Paul McGinley, Darren Clarke and Sergio Garcia – were captains in waiting, and when he saw José-Maria Olazábal wandering around Celtic Manor, he threw him a walkie-talkie and set him to work too. But he saved his masterstroke for the Tuesday evening, three days before the Ryder Cup was due to start. Summoning his side into the European team room, Montgomerie sat them down around a telephone and flicked it on to speakerphone. On the other end of the line was Seve Ballesteros, who was back home in Santander, Spain, recuperating from several operations on a brain tumour. For 10 minutes, the Spanish legend talked to the team, regaling them with stories from his many years of playing in the Ryder Cup and sending them on their way with a message guaranteed to get the blood pumping. "Go get them so hard," he demanded, "that they'll all be caddies in the future."

It was the perfect rallying cry. Ballesteros, after all, was the one man who had done more to sustain and popularize not just the Ryder Cup but the European Tour itself and without him and the character, charisma and genius he brought to the golf course, it's hard to know where both would be today.

The Ryder Cup team would have to wait to act on Seve's instructions as overnight on the Thursday, the Usk Valley was soaked by the kind of biblical rainstorm that left the Twenty Ten course and its much-vaunted, state-of-the-art, £1 million drainage system unable to cope. With the course waterlogged and play suspended for the first time in a Ryder Cup since Valderrama in 1997, suddenly it didn't seem like such a great idea to stage the match in Wales in October. While golf would eventually get under way, with preferred lies in place, the original schedule of play was soon in tatters.

Around the course, meanwhile, the walkways and spectator areas soon became a quagmire and though the Twenty Ten course had been created with the idea of hosting major golf tournaments in mind, with its huge banks creating natural amphitheatres around the greens, the deluge had seen those same banks now become almost impossible to negotiate without the aid of crampons. The *Independent* newspaper reported that over the weekend nine people had fallen and broken their legs in the treacherous conditions – another record that Celtic Manor would rather not hold.

As the rain teemed down in the Vale of Usk, the players did what they could to pass the time. Some played table tennis; some watched television; others played computer games. Poulter, meanwhile, was ambling around the club, furtively capturing some moments on his Smartphone for posterity before posting them on you know where. There was Padraig Harrington caught sleeping on the locker room floor, Rory McIlroy being serenaded by fans and Lee Westwood and Darren Clarke signing some autographs. Ever considerate, he even reached out to his American opponents, all of whom had been banned from tweeting for the duration of the Ryder Cup. "Bubba, I'll send a Tweet out for ya!" he wrote. "Say hello to all your mates!"

With more bad weather forecast over the weekend, a plan was hatched with the agreement of the two captains, and a new schedule of play, with longer sessions, was agreed to try and guarantee a finish on the Sunday. Not that it worked. More rain overnight would delay the start of play until Saturday noon, but even then there was no realistic chance of the Ryder Cup concluding as planned. So three days became four and the Ryder Cup would now finish on a Monday, the first time it had ever done so.

Europe would, eventually, go into the singles with a healthy 9½–6½ lead, while Poulter once more had enjoyed another profitable Ryder Cup, taking two points from three games played with three different partners. Having lost with Ross Fisher to Steve Stricker and Tiger Woods on the first day, he joined forces first with Luke Donald to defeat Bubba Watson and Jeff Overton in the extended Saturday foursomes and then, with Martin Kaymer, beat Phil Mickelson and Rickie Fowler in the fourballs.

Monday would bring sunshine and the waterproofs had finally given way to T-shirts and smiles. The order for the singles had seen Montgomerie place Poulter at fifth in the line-up, pitting him against the 32-year-old from Georgia, Matt Kuchar. It was a strange middle-order position for one so suited to the Ryder Cup as Poulter, who was surely deserving of either a lead or anchor role. Still, it was clear that he was intent on once more delivering for his team, as the vice-captain José-Maria Olazábal explained. "On the Monday I was in the locker room waiting for the players to come out and was giving them encouragement," he says. "I looked at Ian's face – the eyes were the same as they were on Saturday – and I said, 'OK, I don't have to say anything, you're ready.' He looked at me and said, 'Yes, and I can guarantee you a point.' That's Poulter at the Ryder Cup."

True to form, Poulter went out and simply demolished Matt Kuchar, winning 5&4. Yet his result was hardly representative of the European team as a whole. The Americans, traditionally stronger in the singles format, gradually clawed their way back into the match: Steve Stricker beat Lee Westwood; Stewart Cink halved with McIlroy; Dustin Johnson hammered Martin Kaymer; and Tiger Woods dismantled his opponent Francesco Molinari and the course itself, going on a nine-under par run through 11 holes in his comprehensive 4&3 win. Europe were wobbling and when 21-year-old debutant Rickie Fowler somehow snatched a half with the other Molinari, Edoardo, birdieing the final four holes to come back from four down, it seemed as though Montgomerie's team would be found wanting.

The match would hinge on the final singles game left out on the course between Northern Ireland's Graeme McDowell and America's Hunter Mahan. McDowell had become the first British winner of the US Open since Tony Jacklin in 1970 when he lifted the title at Pebble Beach in June. After a career-high year in the game he'd been disappointed when he learned that he would be the last man out, assuming, incorrectly as it transpired, that the match would be over by the time he finished and that his game against Mahan would be largely irrelevant.

He couldn't have been more wrong. With the match score tied at 13½ points apiece, everything depended on McDowell, and when Mahan won the 15th, it left the American just one hole adrift of the Irishman. McDowell would respond magnificently, however, draining a deadweight birdie putt at the 16th to leave himself dormie two up.

Though it had restored McDowell's two-hole advantage, Mahan was still in a position to deprive Montgomerie's Europe of the victory should he win the last two holes – a tied final result, of course, meant that the holders would retain the trophy. Which, as anyone knows, is as good as winning. But the pressure would get to Mahan before it got to McDowell. Faced with a chip up to the green at the 17th, the American duffed it like a weekend hacker, failing even to make the putting surface. With McDowell just five feet away, it meant that Mahan needed to hole his next shot to keep the game alive and, when he missed, admirable effort though it was, he simply strode forward, removed his cap and conceded the game and the match to McDowell and Europe.

After a stop-start week, governed by some wretched weather, the European celebrations would be long and hard, and led, in the main, by Poulter, draped in a cross of St George, and by his Spanish team-mate Miguel Angel Jimenez, who had another of his trademark cigars on the go and was swigging straight from a bottle of Rioja. It had been another astonishing display by Poulter, not least because in Matt Kuchar he had overwhelmed *the* form player on the PGA Tour and duly delivered the point he had publicly promised ahead of the final round of singles. "I said I was going to win, and I did. I love the Ryder Cup, always have. I've watched so many matches over the years: Seve, Colin, Nick Faldo just poured passion into this event," he beamed afterwards. "I love it from the first tee. I love it from the songs. And I love it with all 11 team-mates. It truly is the best tournament in the world, and always will be."

In the papers the following day, among the many photographs printed of the European players celebrating, there was one of Poulter with McDowell on the 17th green, moments after victory had been confirmed. Both men were screaming uncontrollably, with Poulter's manic stare resembling that of a slasher movie villain. It was an image that not only showed what the Ryder Cup meant to him, but one that also scared the living daylights out of his daughter Aimee-Leigh. "She couldn't look at that picture without flinching," he explained later. "She says: 'Daddy, you look very frightening.'"

After the drama and eventual delight of Celtic Manor, Poulter took a well-deserved break, repairing to his home in Florida to see the family and, as it transpired, get up to a little high jinx. Ever the upstart, Ian took to Twitter posting videos of himself and his children eating their breakfast cereal – Cheerios, for the record – out of the Ryder Cup itself, causing outrage and hilarity in equal measure. In a clip he called "Breakfast With The Ryder Cup", Poulter demonstrated how the famous trophy might be utilized in an entirely different manner and presented a step-by-step guide as to how to use it for the most important meal of the day, before grabbing some spoons and tucking in with Aimee-Leigh and Luke.

While undeniably funny, and hardly an act of high treason, not everyone was impressed with the Ryder Cup star's latest online offering. "In some ways it appears disrespectful," said Gary Silcock, then director of golf at The Belfry. "I think taking a drink from it is one thing, to eat cereal with your children is another. It is not in keeping with the traditions of golf – but that's Ian Poulter himself. He does not keep to traditions. It would have been much better if he had not done it."

But while some of the game's traditionalists spat their G&Ts over the lapels of their blazers, little did they know that Poulter was only having a joke with everyone. "The trophy is a replica sent to all the players. It is a nice thing to do. Obviously I wouldn't have dreamt of eating out of the real thing," he told the *Daily Telegraph*, before adding, "champagne perhaps, but not Cheerios."

Comic turns aside, the break would do him the power of good and come November he was finding some of the best form of his career. Indeed, in his regular trip across to Asia and the Middle East, Poulter seemed, at times, to be operating on some higher golfing plane, such was his rich vein of form. After a tie for 13th at the WGC-HSBC Champions in Shanghai, China, he moved on to the Barclays Singapore Open to defend the title he had won from wire-to-wire in 2009. Certainly, the signs that he was somewhere approaching his best were all there. In the second round, for instance, he scorched around the Sentosa Golf Club in an eight-under-par 63, a round that climaxed with a monster birdie putt of around 100 feet at the final hole. Indeed, it was only a final round of 73 that would scupper any chance of overtaking the eventual winner, Australia's Adam Scott, and left him in a tie for sixth.

Clearly, there was precious little wrong with Poulter's game. Indeed, the only issue, it seemed, was whether he could string four good rounds together in succession, a question that he answered emphatically the following week at the UBS Hong Kong Open. Finally, it would prove to be a week where he brought his A-game.

Though the Hong Kong Golf Club was a course tailor-made for low scores, Poulter's assault on it made it look like little more than a glorified pitch and putt. After a 67 in his first round, he then ripped up the course in his second, plundering eight birdies in his last 12 holes and posting a career-best low round of 60. And yet it could have been even better, but for another birdie putt at the 17th that pulled up agonizingly short. Had that putt have dropped it would have been the first official sub-60 round ever recorded in a European Tour event.

It had been a scintillating display by the Englishman, although the fact that he had left a few shots out on the course clearly irked him. "I am happy," he shrugged later, "but slightly disappointed."

A third-round 64, meanwhile, would leave Poulter with a two-shot cushion over his Ryder Cup team-mate Graeme McDowell and even a final round surge by the 17-year-old Italian prodigy Matteo Manassero, who carded a 62, and Yorkshire's Simon Dyson, couldn't deny him another Tour title, his second of the season and the 10th of his career.

Poulter seemed to be in that rarest of states for a professional golfer, where the shot selection and the subsequent execution were working if almost flawlessly and where the ball nearly always did as it was told. Even when the golfing gods conspired to intervene and attempt to put him in his place he seemed able to rise above it all and to carry on as if nothing much had happened. At the European Tour's season-ending Dubai World Championship at Jumeirah Golf Estates the following week, for example, Poulter's encouraging form had showed no sign of abating as he cruised into a share of the halfway lead with Ross Fisher; after a 69 on Saturday, he forged a two-stroke advantage going into the final round.

Come Sunday, Poulter seemed set fair for his first back-to-back wins on Tour but was caught by the Swede Robert Karlsson, who had begun his final round with two birdies and an eagle in his first three holes and then birdied the 620-yard 18th to post a 67 – a score good enough to take him into a play-off with the Englishman, who, in turn, had posted a respectable two-under-par 70 for a total of 274.

Given his match play credentials and his fondness for one-on-one competition, Poulter would start the play-off as favourite. Both players made birdies at the first extra hole, so they continued to the par-five 18th, where the tournament would end in controversial circumstances. A poor approach from Ian with his sand wedge left him with a difficult 30-foot putt for birdie, an error coolly exploited by Karlsson, who arrowed his pitch to within three feet.

But as Poulter marked his ball with his "lucky" platinum and diamond marker adorned with his kids' names, he dropped it. Ordinarily, that would not be a problem, but on this occasion his ball had fallen straight on to his marker, causing it to flip forward; while it only moved about a centimetre closer to the hole, it was sufficient for Poulter to summon over the referee, Andy McAfee, who confirmed that it meant an immediate one-stroke penalty. When he then missed his putt, it meant that Karlsson had two shots from near tap-in range to secure the victory.

It's one of those bizarre rules that appears to make little sense to anybody outside of the game of golf but never ceases to cause confusion and consternation whenever it rears its petty head. After all, it wasn't as if Poulter was seeking to gain any advantage from the situation and if, for example, he had dropped his ball on his marker and it hadn't moved then there would have been no penalty. But for the first time in what had been one of his best seasons to date, Ian's "lucky" marker had not delivered.

It was testament not just to Poulter's increasingly mature attitude on the golf course but the success he had enjoyed in 2010 that he didn't make a huge deal about being the victim of another of golf's minor but maddening rules, even if it did cost him more cash than most people earn in a decade. Yes, it was irritating and yes, it had cost him the chance of the first back-to-back wins of his professional career but there was no real rage, no unedited fury this time. "How frustrated am I?" he said. "Well, it cost me 20 rankings points, a lovely trophy and over half a million dollars. That frustrated."

While all the talk in the sports media was how Poulter's penalty had cost him so dearly, the truth was that it hadn't cost him the title, not really. There was, after all, no guarantee he would have made his putt at the first time of asking, a point proved when he duly missed after the penalty stroke. Besides, the very fact that people were focusing more on his misfortune was actually rather unfair on Robert Karlsson, who had battled back from serious injury and illness to win.

Despite the setback, Poulter took some consolation in the fact that he had, however, once more moved back into the world's top 10, but not before he had taken some obligatory stick via the world of social media. "Poults may not have won the Dubai world championship," wrote his social media sparring partner Rory McIlroy, "but he could be in with a shout for tiddlywinks world championship!"

Irrespective of the occasional petty ruling, for Poulter it had been a season and a year to remember, but success in 2010 was simply part of what had been a remarkable year for European golf. Another Ryder Cup win, a Brit – Lee Westwood – at number one in the world and in Graeme McDowell, the first European winner of a US Open since Tony Jacklin in 1970. It had, unquestionably, been a rare year and one that Poulter, particularly, thought deserved recognition. The European Ryder Cup team did win the Team of the Year award at the BBC Sports Personality of the Year (SPOTY) show, but the fact that some of golf's greatest achievers missed out in the individual category incensed Poulter, not least because one of the performers who finished higher than golf's short-listed candidates, like Westwood and McDowell, was the darts player Phil Taylor, who came in second behind the winner, the jump-jockey AP McCoy. "Darts comes second in the BBC Spoty voting; get a grip," raged Poulter on Twitter. "BBC SPOTY farce, sorry how could Graeme McDowell or Lee Westwood not win. GMac wins a major. Westy World No 1. That's bollox."

Chapter 8
Rage Against the Golf Machine

"I would love some of our commentators to do a day in my shoes with family, gym and practice sessions… They haven't got a f***ing clue how hard we work. They sit on their ass talking crap."

Poulter's response to criticism from Sky Sports commentator Bruce Critchley

If you're a professional golfer, being allergic to grass is something of a drawback. It's like Michael Phelps being allergic to chlorine or Rafael Nadal having a thing about clay. From March through to July each year, when the pollen season was at its highest, Ian Poulter was forced to use a variety of nasal sprays and eye-drops just so he could play. But by the Masters in 2010, his hay fever had reached such uncomfortable extremes that it was beginning to affect his golf game, prompting him to explore just why he was suffering quite so much with the condition.

Having undergone a string of medical tests the results had come back, causing consternation and amusement in equal measure. It transpired that Poulter was allergic to all but one type of grass and all but three kinds of trees which, for a touring pro, wasn't exactly ideal. "Just what a golfer needs, isn't it?" he shrugged. "An occupational hazard, you might say."

It was a rare but not unique condition among other golfers, with fellow sufferers including Australia's 1995 PGA champion Steve Elkington, the Swedish Ryder Cup star Jesper Parnevik – who teed it up at the 1999 Open Championship with two bits of tissue stuffed up his nostrils – and the LPGA Tour star Jill McGill, who would often take similarly drastic action. "Every time I bent over the ball fluid came rushing out of my nose," she once said. "I had no choice but to staunch the flow." For Poulter, though, there was at least some consolation in now knowing why he was feeling the way he was.

At the 2011 WGC-Cadillac Championship at Doral, Miami, soon after, the news of Poulter's newly diagnosed ailment was met with little compassion or commiseration among his contemporaries. The response of Graeme McDowell was typical. "Poults has a face like a bulldog sucking a lemon," he tweeted. "Wonder why?"

But while the hay fever and the allergy may have explained some of his bad form in the spring and early summer, the fact that he was playing poorly, even in January and February, suggested that it wasn't just his ailments that were getting the better of him. Maybe it was the ongoing house renovations or the fact that he was still trying to juggle commitments on both the European Tour and the PGA Tour, but he seemed out of touch and, at times, more than a little niggly. It was one thing being a global golfer, a brand even, but another trying to reconcile the inevitable demands on his time that would entail with still being the golfer he wanted to be.

Poulter's year began with a trip to the Middle East for a trio of European Tour events, the "Desert Swing" as it's known. It would prove to be a memorable visit, not because he won (he didn't) or because he played well (he didn't, for the most part), but because wherever he went he found himself embroiled in one controversy or another. Some were really nothing to do with him. Others were largely self-inflicted. But whatever it was, he seemed to be in particularly spiky mood, with Padraig Harrington's surprise disqualification at the Abu Dhabi HSBC Championship getting the ball rolling – quite literally.

The three-time major winner and Ryder Cup stalwart had been in second place after the first round and had retired for the evening assuming that everything was in order. In television land, however, an eagle-eyed viewer had taken the time out to compose an email and notify the European Tour that he had witnessed the Irishman fail to replace his ball correctly when it moved after he had picked up his marker. The following day, before Harrington's second round was due to start, he was called in to watch a replay of the incident and informed that the penalty for such an offence, given that he signed for an incorrect score at the end of the round, was disqualification.

But if Harrington had taken it on the chin and accepted his punishment without complaint or rancour, Poulter was, for whatever reason, seething. Two weeks earlier, the Colombian golfer Camilo Villegas had been disqualified at the Tournament of Champions in similar circumstances when a viewer phoned in to point out that he had removed some loose pieces of debris after his ball started rolling back toward him after a failed chip shot. Then, Poulter had vented his anger, not at the rules or the rules officials, but at the "snitch" who had called in. "What is wrong with people? Have they got nothing better to do?" he said. "Yes the rules are the rules. It was a mistake on Camilo's behalf. He didn't know he had done wrong, but people calling in? No one likes a snitch."

When Harrington also met the same fate in Abu Dhabi, Poulter was a little more considered, although no less strident in his response, arguing that in the modern era when every shot and statistic is logged, there was actually little need for players to hand in a scorecard after each round, especially not in those high-profile and televised events that these players were competing in every week. "Every shot is visible for everybody to see on television, we have walking scorers, and there are the stats people. Therefore, it's not like you can cheat your score. Therefore, leave the door open if someone has made a mistake," he told a press conference ahead of the Volvo Golf Champions at Bahrain's Royal Golf Club. "If they get a two-shot penalty, they are still in the tournament. The tournament still benefits from having some of the world's best players in the field."

Whichever way you painted it, Poulter had a point, because for all the guts and the glory, the imagination and the genius, golf's predilection for living up to its ultra-conservative image never really went away and the golf rule book with its infinite clauses, infernal sub-clauses and confusing conditions was the bible – the extremely dull bible – by which all followers were governed and constrained. Golf, after all, is a very simple game with a very simple premise, but to know all the rules, inside out and back to front, you'd need to be a qualified rules official or Rain Man.

But if it wasn't the rules or the armchair officials dobbing in the players, it was something else that was getting under Poulter's skin in early 2011. After the first round in Bahrain, he was positively apoplectic when what could have been a promising start to his tournament was ruined not by his own mistakes but by the state of the putting surfaces. "Played great today 35 putts, missed one green. Simply the worst greens I have ever seen and I'm not joking. They are embarrassing," he inevitably wrote on Twitter. "Apparently the

Architect wanted to make a statement with the greens. He did that alright – they are &%$£."

"The Architect" in question, of course, was none other than Colin Montgomerie, the man with whom Poulter had a certain history, and the mere fact that he had chosen not to mention Montgomerie by name suggested that for all the bonhomie on show at Celtic Manor in 2012, there was still a very real enmity between the two. Again, though, Poulter found support from several of his Tour colleagues, some of whom had already seen the course and found the greens wanting. Then world number nine Paul Casey, for example, was under no illusion about the state of the golf course. "I think everybody knows Monty's going to get it in the neck this week," he suggested. "We have a very good course from tee to green. It is in wonderful condition and requires great ball striking. The greens are very, very severe and you're going to hear a lot from the pros maybe complaining about it." Ironically, Casey would cope with Montgomerie's dubious greens far better than Poulter and his four-round total of 268 would see him record his 11th European Tour victory.

The fact that Poulter was making the headlines more for what he was choosing to say on Twitter or in press conferences was the clearest indication that his golf – his day job – was nowhere near its best, and with a missed cut, a tie for 24th and a tie for 63rd, the "Desert Swing" had proved to be a miserable venture. Heading home, he would take a few weeks off to kick back with the family and keep tabs on IJP and the ongoing grand design that was his new house in Lake Nona.

Even when he did find some form, as at the Masters, he found himself frustrated by his inability to convert the chances he had created, a prerequisite for anybody with designs on the Green Jacket. It was especially galling for Poulter, particularly as he was driving the ball as well as he ever had – finding over 82 per cent of the fairways that week – and hitting nearly 70 per cent of Augusta's greens in regulation. His third-round 71 was typical, especially on the back nine, where he manufactured eight genuine birdie opportunities – no small feat on the slick greens of the National Course – but failed to take a single one of them. Then, on the one hole where he didn't fashion a chance, he made a bogey. "I've played some of the best golf I've played in many years," he sighed, as he ended the week with a final-round 73 and a tie for 27th place. "I gave myself lots of chances but the back nine summed up the week."

Of course, Poulter's disappointment would be nothing compared to that of his Ryder Cup team-mate Rory McIlroy. Having entered the final day of the 2011 Masters with a healthy four-shot lead and looking every inch the champion in waiting, the 21-year-old had collapsed in spectacular style around the turn; a car crash 10th hole, where his tee shot found a part of Augusta rarely seen let alone visited, saw him make a triple bogey, followed soon after by a four-putt double bogey on the 12th. Come the end of the round, McIlroy would sign for an ugly 80 to finish 10 strokes adrift of the winner, Charl Schwartzel, in 15th place.

It is one of those inevitable aspects of a professional golfer's career that they will suffer a slump. Of course, it's the very best players who manage to extricate themselves from the mire, and whether it's working on a particular aspect of their game or undergoing major remedial work on their swings – as Nick Faldo did when he disappeared with David Leadbetter in the winter of 1984–85, only to return to action and eventually win six major titles – it is one of the many challenges that face professional golfers as they endeavour to keep pace with the rest of the field.

For Poulter, the issue wasn't with his swing or his putting so much as the fact that he simply wasn't challenging for tournaments and, but for a tie for sixth place at the year-opening Tournament of Champions in Hawaii, he had singularly failed to mount anything like a charge during the early events in his schedule.

Take the WGC-Accenture Match Play Championship at The Ritz-Carlton Golf Club in Marana, Arizona. Twelve months earlier, Poulter had taken the title, beating his compatriot Paul Casey in the final and rising to a career-best world ranking of five in the process. Then, it had been a composed, controlled and consummate performance by him, demonstrating all of the qualities that made him such a fearsome match play performer. But now, as defending champion, he would find himself eliminated in the first round – the first reigning champion to suffer such a fate in nine years – as he was beaten at the first extra hole by the 2009 Open champion, Stewart Cink.

It was a tepid defence of his title made all the worse by repeated run-ins with Stephen Cox, the rules official who was accompanying their game. As both players struggled to find form, the pace of the match slowed considerably, culminating in a tortuous par-three sixth hole, where both men made double bogeys. On the next hole, the players were interrupted by Cox, who had pulled up alongside them in a buggy and asked them to get on with it. But it made little difference and on the eighth, Cox put them on the clock, meaning that one more warning would see both players penalized. Eventually, it would take them a little over four hours to complete the initial 18 holes, which for a two-ball game is painfully slow. The only consolation was that even as a first-round loser Poulter still picked up a cheque for $45,000, which, given that he only played for four hours or so, wasn't such a bad return.

Certainly, there was precious little to suggest that Poulter was about to turn a corner with his golf game and the fact that he had been dumped out of one of his favourite tournaments, playing his preferred format, with barely a whimper must surely have set alarm bells ringing. Worryingly, the slump would continue and he would even miss a cut – at the Ballantine's Championship at Icheon, South Korea – something that was out of the ordinary for a player who prided himself on his ability to hang in there and grind out a score when he needed to.

At times, it seemed as though Poulter was living his life at breakneck speed, traversing the globe and racking up the air miles at an indecent rate, playing here, there and everywhere. And if he wasn't getting his knuckles rapped for slow play then he was being criticized for playing too fast. He simply couldn't win. At the game's unofficial fifth major, The Players Championship, held at Pete Dye's evil masterpiece at Sawgrass, Poulter and his playing partner Dustin Johnson found themselves racing round the course in a bid to beat the fading light – the plan being that by finishing their third round that evening they would avoid having to come back early in the morning to play what was left of it.

Having tackled the infamous island hole 17th, the duo sprinted to the tee on their final hole in a bid to beat the horn that would sound to signal the end of play, and then raced between their shots as they sped down the 18th fairway. As two young men, slim of figure and fleet of foot, it was an impressive display of athleticism and one could only wonder what might have happened had Poulter been paired with Colin Montgomerie or maybe John Daly. But he and Johnson managed to complete their rounds and snuck in just ahead of the hooter, guaranteeing the Englishman a nice lie-in come Sunday and avoiding the prospect of a 5.15am start just to complete one or two holes.

It had seemed an eminently sensible idea on the part of the two players, but not everybody was happy, especially in the NBC commentary box, where the double major winner Johnny Miller openly questioned the pair's antics. "I'm not sure about the etiquette of this," he said, as if Poulter and Johnson were somehow short-changing the galleries, although nobody else seemed to agree with him. "Criticizing [Poulter] for teeing off on the 18th the way he did is unfounded," said the 2008 US Ryder Cup captain Paul Azinger on Twitter. "Every player on Tour would have done the same thing."

Of course, it's one of those bugbears of professional players that experts and analysts can sit in the relative comfort of the commentary box and pass judgement on the players as they go about their business. Sometimes, if the criticism is valid and comes from someone with a track record to back up what they contend, such as, say, Jack Nicklaus, then a player might listen. Often, though, the words fall on deaf ears. When Poulter learned of Miller's comments, his response was more playful than pernicious. "Johnny Miller is only giving me grief because he would have four-putted the 17th green after a casual jog," he said.

Whatever it was about him that irked Miller, it seemed that the 1973 US Open champion was always ready, willing and able to take a swipe at Poulter. In early 2013, for example, during the Hyundai Tournament of Champions set in Kapalua's heavenly Plantation Course in Hawaii, Poulter had backed away several times from a putt on the par-three 11th hole as strong winds battered the course. He sensibly avoided grounding his putter in case the ball moved, an infringement that would have cost him a penalty stroke. But Miller wasn't happy. "You just can't stay over the putt that long, you got to get in there, line it up and hit it," he said, even though the semi-flare on Poulter's ice-white trousers was blowing like the stars and stripes in a hurricane. "He surely doesn't have the Tom Watson attitude so far, he's afraid he's going to hurt himself and that would probably set the game back 20 years… He's just taking way too much time. He's being fairly dramatic here."

For Miller, a commentator whose opinions always seemed to hark back to a golden era of the game (an era which happened to coincide with his peak years as a player), it was fairly predictable, unlike Poulter's response. "Johnny miller," he tweeted, "why don't you come interview me live and say that stuff straight to my face. Was you watching a different channel."

Though Poulter defended himself – and rightly so – Miller was still perplexed when asked about the latest spat he had managed to engineer. "He was being a little overly dramatic and taking extra amounts of time and sort of milking the shots a little bit more just to show it was unfair to play," Miller said. "That was his prerogative, but I thought he was sort of overplaying the whole thing. It got over the edge, no doubt about it. I could see why guys would get a little over the edge wanting not to go on any farther. I don't criticize anybody for that, but it seemed like Poulter… it wasn't anything big. I just said he was being a little dramatic, that's all."

Miller, like so many analysts across sports, is one of those announcers who is hired a) because they have an impressive golf resumé, and b) because they really don't seem to care who they may upset in the course of their commentary. It's the same with the six-time major winner Nick Faldo, whose opinions on CBS's coverage of the PGA Tour are said to be worth $8 million a year to Britain's greatest ever golfer. But like so many other analysts, Miller belongs to a different generation, a bygone era when everything about golf, apart from the object of the game, was different. Presumably, then, Poulter had come to typify everything about the modern game, from the clothes to the haircut to the hard-edged personality. In fact, pretty much all those things that made Miller stand out, back in the mid-1970s.

But it was interesting to see just how frequently Poulter was becoming embroiled in these petty spats. The problem, for the most part, was not merely that he seemed to get under people's skins (and vice versa), but that he was all too ready to respond. But that is his nature and those who take pot shots at him know only too well the publicity bonus they'll garner off the back of any confrontation with him, be it online or otherwise.

Incidents like this, being unnecessary and futile, merely served to distract Poulter at a time when he was plate-spinning like crazy. A cursory look at his schedule in early 2011 reveals a picture of a golfer pulled all over the world by the many demands on his time: Hawaii, Abu Dhabi, Bahrain, Qatar, Arizona, Spain. Factor in the house build, his sponsor and media commitments and it's easy to see how difficult it may have been for him to work on his game.

Indeed, it was telling that his best showing since Hawaii would come at Arnold Palmer's tournament at Bay Hill, just a stone's throw from Poulter's home in Orlando, suggesting that nothing worked better for his game than a few days at home with Katie and the kids. And anyway, he wasn't overly concerned. "I've had spells like this before. I'm not worried," he insisted. "In golf things can turn around very quickly."

Other players, in fact *most* other players, may have sought help from their sports psychologist just to help them through such a comparatively sticky patch. After all, it was Bobby Jones who said that golf was "played mainly on a five-and-a-half-inch course, the space between your ears". It's true. Ask any player, good, bad or ugly, and they'll doubtless say that golf is all in the head. The trouble is, of course, that while recognizing that fact is one thing, doing something positive about it is something else entirely.

Increasingly, though, the game's elite players were all using "mind gurus" to help give them a competitive edge. Luke Donald, for example, climbed up the rankings to become world number one after working with Dave Alred, the man who had also brought out the very best in Jonny Wilkinson and England's rugby union team. The likes of Lee Westwood and Graeme McDowell achieved huge success after working with Dr Karl Morris, while the king of all mind gurus, Dr Bob Rotella, has helped inspire legions of players, from Darren Clarke to Davis Love III, Nick Price to Padraig Harrington. Indeed, Rotella's groundbreaking work with the players – not to mention his multi-million selling books such as *Golf Is Not A Game Of Perfect* and *Putting Out Of Your Mind* – have not just propelled him to the forefront of sports psychology, but also ushered in a new era for professional golf, where the sports psychologist is now an integral part of every player's backroom team. Where once they were viewed with suspicion, cast as charlatans, today they're a key weapon in helping players gain an advantage. It's as Lee Westwood says: "If you get into contention (at a major), you'll find your balls in your throat. The trick is not to choke on them."

But while other professionals sought to eviscerate their minds of what Rotella calls "junk", the notion that Poulter was suffering from issues with his mental fortitude couldn't have been further from the truth. Besides, if there was one thing that he possessed in abundance it was self-confidence and the idea of him hiring a sports psychologist seemed about as logical as employing a plumber to make his trousers. To this day, he steadfastly refuses to employ a sports psychologist, no matter how shaky his form may be, although he's quite willing to help those other players who may need a little fillip. "I've never worked with a sports psychologist. I believe it's in me," he told *GQ* magazine in early 2013. "Anything is possible if you have the right level of concentration and focus. It doesn't matter who you are – you can achieve anything."

While using a swing coach like Leadbetter made sense to Poulter and, indeed, had served him well since he moved to the States, the merest suggestion that he would even consider seeing a sports psychologist, let alone hire one, would be enough to render him incredulous. "Do you honestly think I need a sports psychologist? Are you crazy?" he once said in response to a journalist's question. "Wow! I think people would pay *me* a fortune to be a sports psychologist. That's incredible."

Jamil Qureshi, the official psychologist for the European Ryder Cup team of 2006 and a man who has worked with countless players, from Sergio Garcia to Darren Clarke, agrees. "Psychologists can be unnecessary, but psychology is not," he explains. "Poulter says he does not need a psychologist and I agree with him. The vast majority of people who claim to be golf psychologists in my experience are pretty rubbish. Poulter is a perfect example of someone who has made the most of his talent by thinking the right stuff at the right time. In fact, I'd argue that Poulter's greatest talent is not his technique, but his mindset and attitude. There are many golfers who lost their card last year, who have the talent to be in the top 30 in Europe, the only difference being what goes on behind the eyes."

And, as if to prove a point, Poulter, without a mental coach in tow analysing his every move, headed to the Volvo World Match Play at Finca Cortesin in May. Over the course of a spellbinding week on the Costa del Sol, he not only dragged himself out of his temporary torpor but displayed all the indefatigability that scores of professionals would doubtless pay a small fortune to possess.

It was typically gutsy stuff and, for that matter, classic Poulter match play. All week, he would find himself down to his opponents and all week, he would, through sheer force of will and some brilliant putting under pressure, come through each test. Initially, though, it had seemed as if his malaise might persist as halved matches against the world number one Lee Westwood and Scotland's Paul Lawrie saw him squeeze through to the last 16 for another match against Westwood. This time, though, he would shade it, winning a compelling encounter at the final hole to set up a quarter-final against Francesco Molinari. Poulter would birdie the final three holes of his match with the Italian to overcome a two-hole deficit. He then repeated the trick on the Sunday morning in his semi-final against the big-hitting Belgian, Nicolas Colsaerts, when he came from three-down to win at the 16th hole.

The final would pit Poulter against his Ryder Cup colleague, Luke Donald, a player who also stood poised to overtake Westwood to become the world number one if he could prevail. Quiet and reserved, Donald was the complete antithesis of Poulter. Rarely did he ever become that excited on the golf course. You might get a casual wave of gratitude to the galleries or maybe a quick doff of his visor, but rarely would you see a fist pump and you'd never, ever, witness the kind of wild, primal scream that Ian had a penchant for whenever a vital putt found its mark.

Again, however, Poulter would struggle to impose himself on the match. Three times Donald would ease into a lead but three times Poulter would peg him back. Tenacious and determined, Poulter would cling onto Donald's coat-tails as he threatened to move away and even took a tumble at the eighth, losing his lucky ball marker in the process (it was found and returned by a referee soon after).

But Poulter was not to be denied. With his putter in the kind of prodigious form that would fell the hardiest of opponents he opened up a lead after the turn and reached the 17th hole two up with two to play. His approach to the penultimate hole, meanwhile, would leave him a 10-footer for the victory and somehow, everybody knew it wasn't going to miss. Dutifully, the ball dropped and his name would join a list of previous winners that included Jack Nicklaus, Arnold Palmer and Seve Ballesteros.

It had been a staggering and unpredictable turnaround for Poulter. In the season to date, Westwood and Donald had, by some distance, been the very best players in the world whereas clearly he was not. Now, he had found some form from somewhere and reinforced his claim to be the world's best match play performer. Dedicating his victory to his son Luke, who was back home in Orlando celebrating his seventh birthday, Ian was quite understated in his celebrations. "It's a nice boost. Plenty of questions have been asked of me over the last five months," he said. And now he had answered them all in the best way possible, without even taking to Twitter.

Now back in the world's top 15 players, Poulter's victory had assuaged any fears that those in the game may have harboured about the state of his play. Of course, he himself had no such fears. Butch Harmon, the former coach of Tiger Woods, put it best in 2012. "One of the things I've always loved about Ian Poulter is that people say 'He's not that great a player, he doesn't do anything special, his swing doesn't look that great, he doesn't hit it that great', but he thinks he's the best player in the world. That's why I love the guy… We see this self-belief from the greats. It comes from the inside."

With Volvo's cheque for €566,660 safely in the bank, Poulter's life returned to something approaching normality, which, for the most part, meant spending large chunks of that cash on the ongoing money pit that was the new house in Covent Garden Drive. Another €53,400 gained for a tie for 18th at the BMW PGA Championship at Wentworth the following week would also help to pay for some plug sockets.

Yet the form that had seen him through in the Volvo World Match Play would once more desert Poulter as the effects of all that globe-trotting appeared to catch up with him. At the US Open at Maryland's Congressional Country Club, he shot 75 and 73 to miss the cut by three strokes as Rory McIlroy put the misery of the Masters behind him, setting no fewer than 11 records on his way to victory, including the lowest ever winning total at the event (-16).

Worse was to follow. Trying a different method of preparation for the Open Championship at Royal St George's in Sandwich, Kent, Poulter decided to opt out of the traditional pre-Open event at the Scottish Open and instead indulge his love of all other sports. He had a seat in the Royal Box at Wimbledon to see Andy Murray lose his semi-final to the Spaniard Rafael Nadal; he called in on the

Goodwood Festival of Speed in West Sussex; and he squeezed in a VIP visit to the British Grand Prix at Silverstone too. "You can't hit balls every day of the week. It just doesn't work, that's simple. You're just going to be too tired," he explained. "I forgot my golf and enjoyed the sporting occasions, it's fantastic. It's always good to see the best sportsmen in the world do their job. You get an insight into how they can help you; temperament, body language – all that stuff."

Arriving at St George's, he was feeling enthused and reinvigorated and was happy with just a couple of practice rounds to get used to the golf course. Declaring himself content with his preparations, he told the media that he was "here to win," adding, "My game is good enough."

But it wasn't. Two rounds later, he was on his way home – a second-round 78 sealing his fate – alongside other high-profile casualties such as Lee Westwood, Luke Donald, Padraig Harrington and Graeme McDowell.

Maybe it was the constant globe-trotting catching up with him or perhaps the fact that he just needed a break from an unremitting Tour schedule, but Poulter seemed spent. His decision to try and play both the PGA Tour and the European Tour, something few players have managed to do with any real success, was also jeopardizing his chances of qualifying for the Ryder Cup and, while he could realistically expect to land one of European captain José-Maria Olazábal's two wild card places given his exceptional record in the event to date, it was simply not in his nature to coast along and let other people do him favours.

That said, you couldn't really blame him for taking advantage of some of the rewards that professional golf has to offer. After all, even in an age of austerity where the world was being torn asunder by financial crises, professional golf still seemed to be exempt from much of the suffering. On the PGA Tour, for example, there was the FedEx Cup, a play-offs style competition where players accumulated points over a given series of events and whose eventual winner would receive a staggering $10 million windfall. Not to be outdone, the European Tour had also replaced the old Order of Merit with the Race To Dubai, where the top 15 players at the end of the season contested a bonus pool of $7.5 million. Yes, wherever you looked in golf there was money to be made and, as Poulter was finding out, those Ferraris didn't come cheap.

But this had been a strange and in many ways unsatisfying season for Poulter. Though he had won the Volvo World Match Play, there were precious few other highs and the fact that he had missed the cut in two of the four majors wasn't just uncharacteristic, it was disconcerting too. Finishing 87th on the PGA Tour money list and seeing his world ranking drop from five to 28, meanwhile, was the clearest sign yet that Poulter's game was in the doldrums. The only consolation, it seemed, was that it wasn't a Ryder Cup year.

If you drilled deeper, however, you could see that his form, while undeniably mediocre by his standards, was perhaps not so dire as first thought. Thanks to the PGA Tour's penchant for keeping statistics on everything from birdies to bounce-backs – they'll probably have a divot distance table soon as well – it appeared that, if anything, there was actually reasons for Poulter to be cheerful, even if his results over the year hadn't really suggested as much. In 2010, for example, he was ranked 181st in greens in regulation, having hit 62.47 per cent, but that year, 2011, he had hit 65.58 per cent to climb to 96th. His scoring average had also come down from 71.53 to 70.90 shots per round and while he had lost four yards from his average driving distance he was actually hitting more fairways than he had in 2010.

As ever, though, it was his stellar short game that was keeping him in contention and his scrambling and sand saves percentages continued to be among the best on the PGA Tour. His putting too was clearly helping to keep his rounds together and intriguingly it was those 10–15 foot putts where Poulter had the most success. In 2010, for instance, he had holed just 28.57 per cent putts from that range and languished at 116th in the PGA Tour rankings. Now, though, he was draining almost 40 per cent of them, the most of any player on the Tour.

The putting statistics told their own story. Here was a player who was clearly struggling from tee to green but was determined to hang in there and salvage what he could from each and every round. Put simply, it was professional pride that was pulling him through. "It [this year] has been disappointing, poor," he accepted. "I've played terribly. I've had too much on my mind, too much on my plate. The house-building is stressful and it's the usual story. It costs twice as much and takes twice as long. It becomes expensive fitting it out and expensive on your time… [But] I'm over the disappointments and I'm not going to cry over spilt milk. I'm a decent player and if I go back to basics and work my backside off, I'll be fine."

True to his word, he did just that. Representing England at the Omega Mission Hills World Cup in China with his mate Justin Rose, Poulter endured another one of those slightly surreal weeks where the nonsense of his life away from the course seemed to preoccupy his thoughts. First there were strange pains in his feet cured by a Chinese reflexology expert with "seriously strong hands", then a stiff hand, caused by sleeping in the wrong position. "Woke up this morning with the arcade machine grab hand & couldn't pick up my phone to turn it off," he tweeted, presumably with his good hand. "Slept on the arm, fingers numb. Gutted."

It was clear that once again he was enjoying the challenge of a team event (albeit one with teams of just two). After a strong opening 66 and a solid 69 to follow up, the English pairing were looking to make ground on the leaders but blew it with a 68, just as the likes of Germany (61) and the United States (63) pulled away. "Moving day at the world cup & we moved alright, backwards," he told his Twitter disciples. "Pair of melons. We have gelled like Baileys & Guinness, they don't… Oh well."

However, a sterling 63 in the final round – the lowest round of the day – would be enough to take a tie for second place behind Matt Kuchar and Gary Woodland of the US as well as a hefty cheque for $512,500 to split with Justin Rose.

A week later, meanwhile, at his final event of the year, the JBWere Masters in Melbourne, Poulter provided further proof that reports of his golfing demise had been greatly exaggerated. Shooting four rounds in the 60s, he would record a comfortable three-stroke victory over the local favourite Marcus Fraser and everything from his ball striking to his temperament seemed to be working in harmony. Calm, methodical and in total control, it was the perfect riposte to those who had called into question the Englishman's focus. The win would land him a cheque for $180,000, a place back in the world's top 20 ranked players and the gold jacket that was given to the winner. Certainly, it was an interesting addition to Poulter's wardrobe. Not that he cared. "Winner winner chicken dinner," he tweeted, somewhat bizarrely, "… what a way to finish the year."

If the old year had ended well, the new one began in an even better way for Ian Poulter. At the end of January 2012, he and his wife Katie welcomed another addition to the family as their fourth child, Joshua, was born at a Florida hospital. "Life can't get better,' said Poulter on Twitter, accompanied by some pictures of his newborn son. "You could say I'm a very proud daddy. It's going to be hard leaving to play golf."

It was especially hard when he had to head over to Arizona, a few days later, to play in arguably the worst named tournament in professional golf: the Waste Management Open. But travel he did, leaving behind his ever-increasing brood as he sought to build on the change in form and fortune he had enjoyed in Australia.

Chapter 9
His Miracle at Medinah

@IanJamesPoulter
I've had enough of twitter for now. So many F#%€ing idiots. Time out. I'm tired of blocking myself. I'm letting someone else block the pricks @IanJamesPoulter *99% of you guys I will be back soon and you guys are great thank you. To the 1% of you jealous low life scum, get a job & a life.* April 23, 2013 and Ian Poulter announces a break from Twitter. Eight days later he was back.

Whatever one may feel about Poulter and his approach to golf and life more generally, one could never accuse him being anything other than his own man. Whereas players like Luke Donald are naturally circumspect, going about their business with minimum fuss and adept at circumnavigating those press questions designed to trip them up, Poulter says what he likes and, for the most part, likes what he says.

In days gone by, his only outlet would have been a press conference or perhaps a television or newspaper interview. Today, though, he not only has his Twitter account, but almost 1.5 million followers hanging onto his every word, some of which aren't always well chosen or suitable for younger fans. It's this platform, though, that enables him to talk about anything from fashion to football, cars to golf clubs. And it's a responsibility that can weigh heavily on his mind. Today, virtually the first thing Poulter does when he wakes in the morning, after the obligatory press of the snooze button, is to grab his phone and check what's happened on his Twitter feed during the night. It is, by his own admission, an "addiction", a compulsion that he can't quite get a handle on, much as he would like to. "I need to stop. I can't help it," he said recently, with all the desperation of a junkie on the edge. "I read every single reply. Ninety-nine per cent of them are positive."

But it is, however, an instant and sometimes potent weapon to vent his spleen and respond to the critics. In late February 2012, for example, Poulter had travelled west to Tucson, Arizona, to take part in the WGC-Accenture Match Play Championship. With a win in the event in 2010, and as the reigning Volvo World Match Play champion, his formidable record (and reputation) in the head-to-head format had marked him out as one of the pre-event favourites. However, his first-round exit at the hands of the little-known Korean Sae Bang-Moon had many observers scratching their heads, not least because the margin of victory – 4&3 – was so large. In the Sky Sports commentary box, the veteran analyst and former Walker Cup player Bruce Critchley openly questioned Poulter's focus, suggesting that he was perhaps spending more time on some of his extra-curricular activities, such as his clothes label, than on his golf game.

It was a remark and an opinion that, while pointed, hardly warranted the response it received. Frustrated by his premature exit and the way he had played, Poulter characteristically took to Twitter. "I would love some of our commentators to do a day in my shoes with family, gym and practice sessions," he countered. "They haven't got a F&@ "£% clue how hard we work. They sit on there [sic] ass talking crap. That's really difficult… Well Bruce Critchley talks complete bollox most of the time anyway. Sorry sky sports viewers for having to listen to his crap every week."

Grammatical, syntax and spelling errors aside, it was a stinging attack on the man known as "The Colonel", but it wasn't as though Poulter was saving all his vitriol for Critchley. No, he had plenty left over for himself too. "That was simply rubbish, five bogeys, I beat myself," he grumbled. "I wouldn't have given many a good game today. It's a shame. I love Match play. If I'm ever happy in defeat that day will be the last day I ever hit a golf ball. I will retire. I hate losing and hopefully always hate it. I am a bad loser. I've never known a good one."

Obviously, Critchley's comments had caught him after a bad day at the office, but it was still hard to imagine any other golfer reacting in quite the same way. Yet the commentator wasn't the only figure in the game who felt that Poulter's focus perhaps wasn't what it should be. Even his number one fan and the man who had picked him for the 2008 Ryder Cup at Valhalla, Nick Faldo, got caught up in the debate, suggesting that it wasn't just his fashion range that was getting in the way. "Poults has just got too much going on, in my view,' he told Derek Lawrenson, golf correspondent of the *Daily Mail*. "He's got the house in Orlando, which has taken [ages] to build and he must have lost a fortune on it given the way the market has gone. He and his wife have just had their fourth child. He's got the worry of keeping his clothing company afloat and then there's the fact he's always tweeting like crazy. I watched him on the practice ground at the Accenture last week and there he was, bouncing away and tweeting furiously instead of putting in some quality time on his game. Was it any wonder he was all over the place, his feet flying everywhere, and lost heavily in the first round? He's supposed to be the match play specialist, but you can't be that without putting quality time in on the range. If he wants advice from the caring NF [Nick Faldo], it would be to end his tweeting obsession and put in that quality time."

While Faldo's comments went much further than Critchley's in bringing into question everything from Poulter's burgeoning family to the perilous position of property prices in the Orlando area, strangely they didn't garner the same scathing response that Poulter reserved for the 70-year-old commentator. Yes, he leapt on Twitter again, but there was none of the filth or the fury he'd aimed at Critchley, nor was there any personal reference to Faldo himself:

"I'm honoured that people are talking [about the fact] that I'm not working hard enough on my game. I have to answer that question, though. I have never worked harder than I am right now, not only on my game but on my health and fitness. There are areas of my game which we have looked at, and are making big improvements on. It's just a case of them coming together. This game has a funny way of showing hard work sometimes but it is showing and it will show very soon. Trust me, I will deliver like I promised in the Ryder Cup and like I always do. The day to start worrying is when I do. That is no time soon. I will deliver (the postman)."

Rather than tackle Faldo's concerns via social media, Poulter then opted to use the quaint medium of conversation to talk the issue through with his former Ryder Cup captain. Faldo assured his charge that he had been misquoted in the piece, a line that Poulter swallowed in its entirety as he, somewhat ironically, rattled off yet another Tweet: "Don't panic complete false alarm I spoke to Faldo last night and he was totally misquoted, as per normal the papers can write what they like."

But was Faldo actually "misquoted"? Not so, says the journalist who spoke to him. "The truth of the matter is not only was there a voice recorder sitting on the table between Faldo and myself but also a photographic witness to the whole conversation," explains Derek Lawrenson. It's a story given more credence by the fact that after Poulter made his Tweet, Faldo had followed it up with one of his own, claiming that he had been misquoted when he had said that he had been misquoted. Things were getting silly. "Spoke with IJP and my advice is same," he wrote, "if postman believes he's giving 100 per cent let's see if he delivers."

What had started out as a casual remark by Bruce Critchley on Sky Sports was fast turning into a farce and the fact that it was being played out in the virtual world of social media just seemed to make it all the more ridiculous. Increasingly, though, it seemed as though Faldo had a point, especially when it came to tweeting. No sooner had one Poulter Tweet been dispatched than another would arrive. Often they were funny or informative. Sometimes they were useful, but occasionally they merely served to get him into more hot water. Moreover, he himself had readily admitted in interviews that the ongoing and protracted construction of his new house in Orlando had in some way contributed to what was a less than satisfactory season in 2011. "It's my house," he said at the HSBC Champions tournament in Shanghai in November 2011, "and whether it's a plug socket or the smallest furnishing, I have to make the final decisions. It's my house – I don't want someone else to choose something for it. That's a time-consuming project and it eats away at time when I could be doing other stuff. It has been very stressful. It has cost twice as much and taken twice as long as I thought. It becomes expensive, not only on your house but also on your time."

Despite the all too regular spats, quarrels and somewhat heated exchanges, Twitter remains Poulter's preferred mouthpiece and if that means someone takes exception every now and then so be it. It is, as Poulter contends, the inevitable consequence of being a free spirit in an inherently conservative game. "I give people what I feel every day. If I'm ------ off, I'll tell you. If I've had a great day, I'll tell you I've had a great day. If Arsenal have lost, I might be frustrated. I kind of give enough, so that it gives a whole picture. Some people get offended if I've bought a new car, or have something delivered, and then decide to show it."

Two years and nine months from when the ground was first broken, the home that had long occupied the thoughts not just of Poulter and his family but teams of builders and even six-time major winners, was finally ready to move into. Situated on Covent Garden Drive in Lake Nona, the same gated community that also housed Poulter's Ryder Cup colleagues Sergio Garcia, Justin Rose, Peter Hanson and Graeme McDowell, it was 10,000-plus square foot of all-white, modernist design, twice the size of their old house and at odds with most of the faux Tuscan buildings that exist on the estate. And while he may not have pointed brickwork or laid the pipes, it was, thanks to his personal involvement and exacting attention to detail, very much the house that Ian built, right down to the fact that it had wooden floors throughout as carpets weren't great for his hay fever. "I designed the house around my lifestyle," he explained. "The gym overlooks the kitchen and the pool so if I'm in the gym I can keep an eye on the kids in the pool. If I'm in my games room, I can still look into the pool. It's all about lifestyle. Every detail – the handles on the kitchen doors, the design of the table in the kitchen, the design of the kitchen itself, the wine storage areas, picking the stone – I designed everything."

But while the house itself was ideal for Poulter and his ever-expanding family, he seemed to take particular delight in the garage. A six-bay building bigger than many apartments it also featured a $3,000 lift in the middle bay so he could keep his ultra-rare Ferrari FF (customized with the same tartan he uses in his designs for IJP) off the ground and in tip-top condition. The cars, of course, are Poulter's passion. He has lots of them, but it's the Ferraris that make him weak at the knees. Not only does he have a (hypoallergenic) labradoodle called Enzo (he also has a dog called Bentley) but he once declared that his tour of the Ferrari HQ in Maranello, Italy was "one of the most memorable moments of my life". Even when he came over to the UK in December 2012 for the BBC's Sports Personality of the Year Awards, Poulter couldn't help himself, taking a detour to Tom Hartley Cars in Swadlincote, Derbyshire, and forking out £650,000 on an ultra-rare 1984 Ferrari 288 GTO. Shipping back to Florida would cost extra, however. Most people leave London with a memento. A miniature Big Ben perhaps, or maybe a snowstorm of Tower Bridge. Not Ian Poulter.

It's these conspicuous displays of wealth – he once tweeted a picture of his car lift, for example, complete with his Ford GT on top and his Ferrari California underneath – that seem to grate with some people, especially in such austere and uncertain times. "I'm not doing it to show off," he insisted in an interview with the *Daily Telegraph*'s Oliver Brown in 2011. "I'm just giving you a picture of what's happening in my life. Most people find it interesting. They don't normally get to see that kind of stuff – they only get the TV perception.

"My flooring from Italy arrived. I tweeted a picture about that and got a quick-fire response. 'That's so disrespectful', 'You're a disgrace', 'It's Comic Relief Day, shouldn't you be more considerate?' 'Wouldn't you rather be giving, rather than just bragging?' I didn't do it for that reason. I'm just giving you an insight."

And therein lies the difference. It is Poulter's decision to publish these things, to throw them out to the watching world, that differentiates him from those players who live equally extravagant lifestyles but choose to keep them under their sponsored visors. Take Darren Clarke. What do you know about him? He likes a Guinness, right? And a glass of red wine? Did you know that he's had 15 Ferraris, three Lamborghinis and a wide assortment of Jaguars, Bentleys, Mercedes, BMWs and Porsches in his career? Or that the most cars he's ever owned at the same time was seven? He's had a private jet too, worth £12 million, something Poulter has yet to sign a cheque for. "Do I want the aeroplane? I'd love one," he said. "Do I want a boat? Yeah... Do I want to become a billionaire? Sure."

Spring became summer and Poulter's form was solid if not spectacular. At Augusta, so long one of his favourite hunting grounds, he had been there or thereabouts throughout the week as Bubba Watson, the unorthodox and swashbuckling left-hander from Bagdad, Florida, blazed his way into the history books with a performance that had amazed everyone who watched it. While he had much in common with Poulter in terms of his personality – they were both frank, fearless and flamboyant – their games were markedly different, not least because Watson, with his homegrown swing that defied pretty much all of the coaching manuals, was prodigiously and ridiculously long. A case in point was the hole that won him the play-off against South African Louis Oosthuizen. At the par-four 10th – the second play-off hole – Watson had pulled his drive into the trees, leaving him 155 yards to the pin with no obvious shot. Or at least that's what most people assumed.

Instead, he sized up the situation and with a gap wedge in his hand somehow managed to hook a shot off the pine straw, out of the trees and onto the green, just 12 feet from the hole. A successful putt later and Watson was the Masters champion.

Poulter, meanwhile, had given it a good go in his final round, reaching the turn in a scintillating 33 only to see his challenge falter and culminate in a three-putt triple bogey at the final hole. His finish – he was seventh – was his best yet but still disappointing, especially given his promising front nine and the fact that the Masters was perhaps the one major above all the others that suited his game. It was a shame too, because his canary-yellow shoes would have gone nicely with the Green Jacket.

Still, the signs that Poulter's form was returning were undeniable. In the Open Championship at Royal Lytham & St Annes, he finished like an express train, rattling in a 67 to give him a tie for ninth place while in the final major of the year, the PGA Championship at Kiawah Island, he would tie for third as his Ryder Cup colleague Rory McIlroy won his second major at a canter.

His return to form would come as a huge relief for the European Ryder Cup captain, José-Maria Olazábal. Though Poulter would fail to make the Ryder Cup team as of right – partly because of his form and partly because of his schedule – almost everyone on the game expected him to be one of Olazábal's two wild card picks and the fact that he was now playing the kind of golf to merit a place simply made the decision that much easier.

Besides, Poulter's pedigree went before him. Under Nick Faldo at Valhalla, where he won four out of five points and again at Celtic Manor, where he won three points from four matches, Ian had demonstrated not just his appetite for team competition but his suitability for the cut and thrust of a tournament as fiery as the Ryder Cup. Indeed, as the top European points scorer in those events and a player who had a 100 per cent record in his singles matches, it came as no surprise that Olazábal would select him as one of his wild cards for the match at Medinah, along with the promising young Belgian Nicolas Colsaerts.

Certainly, Poulter couldn't have had any more respect for his captain. On the Saturday evening at Valhalla in 2008, for example, Olazábal, as Nick Faldo's vice-captain, had taken centre-stage in the locker room and talked to the European team about what the Ryder Cup meant to him. Personal, passionate and extremely eloquent, the Spaniard had transfixed the team as they sought to overturn a two-point deficit. On the face of it, it was just a motivational team talk but for many of the players, including Poulter, it was the moment when Olazábal all but rubber-stamped his selection as captain for the 2012 match. Soon after, Ian would recall that lock-down in the locker room and make his predictions for the 2012 Ryder Cup. "The dream scenario for 2012?" he said. "Europe to be defending, Ollie for captain, and Seve back in full health there as his vice."

Poulter was close but, tragically, one element of his prediction failed to materialize. On May 7, 2011, Seve Ballesteros, the man who had done so much to help transform the Ryder Cup from an insignificant sporting anachronism to one of the biggest and most compelling contests in the world, had passed away, his battle with a brain tumour finally coming an end.

As the world mourned his passing, it seemed fitting, then, that
the European team would be led by the player who had been by his
side in so many thrilling Ryder Cups in years gone by: his pupil,
compatriot and friend, José-Maria Olazábal. Here was a player who
had the respect of all of his team, a man whose record in professional
golf, and especially the Ryder Cup, preceded him.

Olazábal was the model captain: eloquent, affable and
deferential. While all the pre-event talk between him and his
opposite number Davis Love III followed the well-trodden route of
the two teams enjoying a healthy and friendly competition while
at the same time maintaining the rich traditions and heritage of
Samuel Ryder's brainchild, it would be Poulter – who else? – who
would light the blue touch paper. "This event is unique," he told a
press conference. "I hate to say we don't get on for three days, but
there is that divide – and it's not that we don't like each other. We
are all good friends, both sides of the pond, but there's something
about Ryder Cup which kind of intrigues me. How can you be
great mates with somebody, but, boy, you want to kill them in
Ryder Cup?"

It spoke volumes about Poulter's confidence and self-belief that
he would not only choose to make such a provocative statement
but to do so ahead of a Ryder Cup in Chicago, one of the most
notoriously boisterous sports cities in the world. If there was any
doubt about the kind of reception he was going to receive from
the home galleries at Medinah, now he could be sure that it would
be far more hostile than he could ever have imagined or, knowing
Poulter, hoped for.

If the Englishman's comments were designed to stoke the flames
then they had succeeded. Even the nice guys in the US team started

to wade in. Take Brandt Snedeker, the recent winner of the $10 million prize in the 2012 FedEx Cup. "I'm very, very competitive," insisted the world number 10. "People don't get that because I'm polite. But I'm going to try to beat their brains in as bad as I can."

Of course, it is one of the quirks of the Ryder Cup that within days of this most fevered and partisan event ending, where accusations, allegations and brickbats are often hurled in the heat of battle, most of the players will, inevitably, line up against each other once more in a Tour event. Remarkably, though, none of the animosity or vitriol ever seems to endure. Friendships and working relationships are almost immediately restored and the element of competition returns to a more individual and selfish focus.

But if Olazábal and Love had been the very epitome of decency and sportsmanship in the build-up to the match, the sudden and inevitable manner in which matters had taken a trashy turn for the worse merely served to increase the anticipation ahead of the matches. Come the first day, as 30,000 fans lined the first hole, it was clear that this was going to be a very raucous Ryder Cup.

Initially, there would be little to separate the two teams as the opening morning's sessions of foursomes were shared, thanks to Poulter and Justin Rose taking the fourth and final game with a relatively straightforward 2&1 win over Tiger Woods and Steve Stricker. But the early promise would be short-lived. Come the afternoon, the USA, buoyed by some frenzied support, took the game to the Europeans. It was so wild that Bubba Watson even had the crowd cheering during his tee shot at the first hole. It seemed to work, though, as Watson and his partner Webb Simpson were carried along on a wave of patriotism, and ran out 5&4 winners over Paul Lawrie and Peter Hanson.

The victory would set the scene for a successful spell for the States and, with Poulter surprisingly omitted from the session, the USA took a deserved 5–3 lead into day two. Matters deteriorated still further on Saturday morning when, again, the US team would be in scintillating form, with Keegan Bradley and Phil Mickelson the pick of the bunch as they crushed Luke Donald and Lee Westwood – two men who had both been the world number one in the previous two years – 7&6. The pins were being peppered and the putts dropping from everywhere. Sadly, though, it wasn't Olazábal's team who were doing it.

The scoreline at the end of the morning session would make for depressing reading for the visitors – they were now down by eight points to four – and the only bright spot was the continued resistance of Poulter who, at times, seemed to be waging a one-man war against an entire nation. Take that opening match of the morning foursomes, where he and his partner Justin Rose were drawn against the reigning US Open champion Webb Simpson and the 2012 Masters champion Bubba Watson. After Watson's antics on Friday, when he had whipped the home crowd into a frenzy, all eyes were now on Poulter to see how he would handle the hostility of the first tee. He didn't disappoint. With the honour, he just stepped forward, teed up his ball and, with a causal wave of his hand, began to get the European contingent of the galleries going, carrying on until the volume had reached the deafening level he was seeking. It was only then that he decided to take his tee shot. Following behind, Watson simply smiled. It was a tacit acknowledgment from the Masters champion that here was a player who could not only play him at his own game but actually take it that bit further. Not to be outdone, though, Watson once more led the home fans into near delirium. "USA! USA! USA!" they bellowed, as their stars and stripes' fluttered in the breeze. "It was a great moment," said Poulter later. "Bubba was always going to do it and I didn't want to be in that situation where he got that one up on us."

Even for the Ryder Cup, where most of the normal etiquette of professional golf seems to take a brief vacation, this was unprecedented. It was raw, raucous and more like a football match than a golf competition. Golf's golden rule of silence – the omnipresent "Quiet Please" sign wielded by the marshals – hadn't just been ignored, it had been run out of town.

Of course, if you've ever been to a Ryder Cup you'll already know that the atmosphere is unlike that of any other golf tournament. Yes, the infamous 16th hole at the Phoenix Open has its fair share of rowdiness but nothing quite compares to the heat of a Ryder Cup match. Even if the closest you've got to one is watching it on television, you'll still get a sense of just how huge a spectacle the event has become. It can be noisier than NASCAR. "It's totally different to anything else in golf," explains Sergio Garcia. "When you play in the Ryder Cup and you see and hear the crowd and the energy they bring to the event, it's second to none."

You suspect that certain players, like Poulter and Watson, would like nothing more than for professional golf to be like this all the time, a game where boisterous interaction with the crowd is part and parcel of the challenge. However, it appeared neither player was totally at ease with it – Poulter carved his drive into the bunker on the left of the fairway and Watson almost followed him in, getting a lucky bounce to pop over the sand and nestle in the rough.

But the showdown suited Poulter perfectly. While other players would step away from a shot if so much as a crisp packet drifted into their eye-line 150 yards down the fairway, Ian positively thrived on the heat of the battle and the noisier and more confrontational it got, the more he seemed to play up to it.

Not that Poulter's example had exactly inspired Europe so far. Indeed, Poulter and Rose would register Europe's only point on that Saturday morning, their narrow one-up victory being the only crumb of comfort from another crushing session.

It wasn't as though José-Maria Olazábal's European team had played badly, far from it, but they had simply been overcome by a rampant American team intent on seizing back the Ryder Cup on their home soil. Davis Love III's men seemed to be the perfect golfing machine. Here was a side, so long castigated for being an assembly of 12 individuals rather than a "team", who were playing almost flawless golf. Everywhere you looked within their ranks, there were players rising to the challenge in front of them. The Ryder Cup was slipping out of Europe's hands and Olazábal and his charges seemed powerless to prevent it.

There was little respite during the afternoon fourballs. Justin Rose and the Italian Francesco Molinari (playing his first game in the 2012 event) were destroyed 5&4 by Watson and Simpson, while Dustin Johnson and Matt Kuchar won at the last against Nicolas Colsaerts and Paul Lawrie. With two fourball games to go, Europe was six points behind and Sunday was already looking like being one almighty wash-out. Sergio Garcia, a Ryder Cup veteran at just 32, and his trusty partner Luke Donald, eked out a point by inflicting the third defeat of the week on the partnership of Woods and Stricker, but it seemed to be of little consolation, not least because Poulter and Rory McIlroy were two down through 12 holes against Zach Johnson and Jason Dufner, and surely heading to defeat.

But something happened in the fading light at Medinah on that Saturday evening, something magical. At the lucky 13th hole, McIlroy rolled in a snaking 18-foot downhill putt to reduce the deficit to one and from then on, Poulter's putter took over. Throughout the remaining five holes, he played golf like a man possessed by some higher power. He would birdie each and every one of them, repelling the Americans at every opportunity. By the 15th, the match was all square. By the 16th, Europe were one hole to the good. And by the time Poulter holed out at the 18th, the duo had completed the back nine in just 29 shots and another point, a wholly improbable one at that, had been won by Europe.

In the press conference, Poulter was at a loss to explain what had just happened or, indeed, why it had happened. "I don't know. But I mean, it comes from within," he shrugged. "And you know, if we can do anything to get this trophy in this position, and Seve is looking down on us, then you've got to do what you've got to do."

It was clear from the way that Poulter was playing, especially in the face of a boisterous and often unforgiving local crowd, that here was a player who not only seemed more suited to the camaraderie of team golf but one who thrived on the hostility. Put simply, when the going got tough, Ian Poulter got going.

From what would surely have been a scene of desolation and despair just an hour earlier, the European team's locker room was now remarkably buoyant. Perhaps it was a little misplaced given that they still had a mountain to climb but those two points, stolen in the fading light, had given Olazábal's players some hope. History and logic seemed to be against them, however. Only once before in the long and rich history of the Ryder Cup had a team managed to overturn such a huge deficit when, in 1999,

Ben Crenshaw's American team (including Davis Love) stunned Mark James's European side at a frenzied Brookline County Club in Massachusetts. But now, thanks to Poulter's heroics, they had a chance, albeit an extremely slim one. But this was the Ryder Cup, an event that turns a fine line in too-close-to-call contests and specializes in the seismic. And besides, the Europeans would be wearing Seve's colours – navy blue – on Sunday.

Predictably, Olazábal would front-load his singles order with his strongest players – but then he had no choice. Indeed, the only surprise was that he didn't send Poulter out first, choosing instead to put out the European team's hero of the hour in the second game against Webb Simpson.

For Europe to have any chance, however, it was imperative that everything went to plan. But while the team had gone to bed on Saturday night fully focused and entirely aware of just what was expected of them on the final day, what they hadn't banked on was one of their key members, the world number one Rory McIlroy, oversleeping and very nearly missing his tee time. As the European team tried to locate their star turn, the young Irishman eventually turned up at the course, courtesy of a police escort by Pat Rollins, the deputy chief of police in Lombard, with just minutes to spare before his match with Keegan Bradley was due to start, with no time to practise and barely enough to apologize to his bewildered skipper.

Panic over, Europe's challenge began in earnest and slowly, the scoreboard started to turn European blue. It would be a couple of hours, however, before anybody dared to think that maybe, just maybe, something incredible was about to occur. Perhaps the key match and the moment when the Europeans really believed that they had a genuine chance of at least retaining the Ryder Cup came in the fourth match out, where Poulter's pal, Justin Rose, faced the four-time major winner Phil Mickelson. It would prove to be an epic encounter. Within two holes, Rose was two up only for Mickelson to peg him back and square the match by the fifth hole. Try as he might, Rose could not shake Mickelson off and the American left-hander took the lead at the 14th hole, maintaining his advantage through the 16th, where Rose had to hole a 10-footer just to stay one down with two to play.

At the par-three 17th, where the players hit over the crowd and across the water to the putting surface, Mickelson's tee shot would find the bank of rough on the high side of the green, while Rose was to find the green but leave himself a downhill 40-foot putt. Predictably, Mickelson would conjure up another slice of magic, chipping the ball down on to green, toward the water, and then wheeling away as it got ever closer to the hole, fully anticipating that it would drop into the hole. But brilliant though the shot was, it still stayed out and as Mickelson tapped in, it seemed that another hole would slip by for Rose. Yet the putt that he made, under the most incredible pressure, was arguably the shot of the 2012 Ryder Cup. Down the hill it meandered, turning left to right, before dropping, at perfect pace, into the hole. As Rose celebrated with a low-slung fist-pump, Mickelson, one of the game's true gentlemen, smiled and nodded his approval as he walked off to the 18th tee. It was a lovely touch from the San Diegan and proof that for all the trash-talk and brickbats the mutual respect between the players, or at least most of them, never really evaporated in the heat of the battle.

With Rose back in the game and now guaranteed at least half a point, the match would go down the last. It was clear that nerves were getting the better of both men. Rose pulled his drive left, Mickelson overshot the green with his approach and after the American chipped up close it left Rose, somewhat incredibly, with a 12-foot putt for victory. Moments later, he duly rolled it in and snatched a priceless victory from what had appeared to be an inevitable defeat. It beggared belief.

It was just the fillip the visitors needed. Sensing their opportunity, the momentum swung in Europe's favour as one by one, they seemed to reel in their opponents, turning the scoreboard into a sea of blue. Poulter would register another win, beating Webb Simpson two up to end the event with a 100 per cent record and, you would think, cement his place for the 2014 Ryder Cup at Gleneagles (irrespective of what he does or doesn't do in the qualification stakes) and, in all likelihood, guarantee a shot at the captaincy in the future as well. In the wake of Poulter's stellar performances, his team-mate Lee Westwood even suggested they should change the qualification rules for the next Ryder Cup so that it became "nine qualifiers, two captain's picks and Poults."

The points were coming thick and fast, and Olazábal's singles strategy seemed to be paying dividends. Luke Donald beat the USA's rabble-rouser-in-chief Bubba Watson, Rory McIlroy overcame Keegan Bradley despite his late arrival and the rejuvenated Paul Lawrie eased past Brandt Snedeker 5&3.

With two games left out on the golf course, the scores stood at 13–13 and the unthinkable had now, incredibly, moved into the realms of possibility. When Martin Kaymer rolled in a testing six-foot putt to beat Steve Striker at the last hole, it meant that Europe had retained the Ryder Cup and still had a chance of winning it outright, if Francesco Molinari could pinch a half-point from his match with Tiger Woods in game 12.

Chapter 9

With the celebrations already underway and the whoopin' and hollerin' of the home crowd now conspicuous by its absence, it came down to a putting contest between Molinari and Woods. When the American pulled his par-putt, he immediately conceded his opponent's to give Molinari and Europe the half point they needed to win outright, by 14½ points to 13½. With just a half point to show from his four matches, it had been another wretched Ryder Cup week for Woods but the fact that he conceded Molinari's putt to give Europe outright victory, rather than make him putt and risk missing it, was an act of sportsmanship that showed real class given the circumstances.

It had been a breathtaking and, in the end, quite preposterous turnaround. Europe had won eight of the 12 singles matches and staged the most incredible comeback, not just in the Ryder Cup but in the wider world of sport. Led by Olazábal and inspired by Ian Poulter's heroics, they had, to use a boxing analogy, picked themselves off the canvas and won in the dying moments of the final round. But more than that, it had been a fitting tribute to the memory of Seve Ballesteros, a player who had been known for his huge heart, his indomitable spirit and almost miraculous powers of recovery.

"Seve taught me one thing above all else," José-Maria had said at the beginning of the week. "Never give in, never quit, anything is possible in this game." It was true, and nobody on the Ryder Cup team heeded that message more than Ian Poulter.

It was interesting then that Olazábal sought out Poulter among the hullabaloo, pulling him close and whispering something in his ear. Visibly moved, Poulter embraced the Spaniard. Later, when he was asked what Olazábal had said to him, all Ian would divulge was that it was "very special" and that whatever had been said would stay between the two of them.

In the revelry that ensued there was a poignant and hugely emotional moment when, faced with the BBC's cameras, the victorious European team captain broke down and, with tears running down his cheeks, turned his eyes to the sky. It was a silent but heart-rending tribute to Olazábal's compatriot, friend and mentor, Seve Ballesteros, who had passed away before he could see his Ryder Cup partner follow in his footsteps and lead the European team into battle at Medinah.

Now, having watched his team overturn what appeared to be an insurmountable four-point deficit to snatch the unlikeliest of victories, the occasion and, perhaps, the realization of what his team had managed to achieve finally hit home. The following day, the world's media, collectively bewildered by what had happened, had almost universally taken to calling the match "The Miracle of Medinah" and the idea that Seve had somehow intervened on that Sunday afternoon was hard to ignore.

But for all the European jubilation, it was a bitter pill for the United States – and especially US captain Davis Love III – to swallow. Two weeks after Medinah, he would compete in the McGladrey Classic, the tournament he hosts in Sea Island, Georgia. Paired with him on the Friday was 2007 Masters champion Zach Johnson, a member of his defeated team. As the two strolled up the final fairway, smiling and waving to the crowd, Johnson stopped in his tracks and turned to Love. "Can I ask you a question?" he said, all stony-faced.

"Sure," shrugged Love.

"Are we ever going to get over it?"

Chapter 9

Love took a moment before responding. "No, we're not going to get over it," he suggested, "but they will be some of the best memories of your life – until you remember that we lost."

***

After a 10-day break at his new home in the Bahamas, where he kicked back, sipping champagne and, bizarrely, ordering 19 new televisions for his new Florida mansion, Poulter returned to Tour action at the BMW Masters at Shanghai's Lake Malaren Golf Club in China. In addition to a nagging throat infection and a general feeling of lethargy – perhaps the inevitable comedown after the highs of Medinah – he was finding the task of readjusting to the day-to-day demands of tournament golf less than inspiring. "Almost three weeks on and, honestly, I still haven't completely recovered, either physically or emotionally," he told the *Daily Telegraph*. "It'll be tough to reacclimatize. There'll be no adrenalin rush, no excitement from the crowd, no team-mates to high-five…"

Even though it was several weeks after the Ryder Cup, all the talk, still, was of what had happened at Medinah and Poulter's admission that he had been reliving the events "in slow motion in his mind" surely typified how the other European players were feeling about the greatest Ryder Cup of all time. The manner of the victory had clearly given the entire European Ryder Cup team an almighty fillip, as nine of the top 14 finishing places in Shanghai were taken by members of Olazábal's side. Poulter finished fourth, while the only man who didn't win any points at Medinah, the Swede Peter Hanson, went on to win the title. Even captain Olazábal got in on the act, rolling back the years to take a creditable 35th place.

Soon after, there was a chance to renew some Ryder Cup acquaintances (and rivalries) at Greg Norman's Franklin Templeton Shoot-out in Naples, Florida, as Poulter – the only player from the European team present – paired up with Dustin Johnson in the better ball tournament, alongside other pairings that included five of the American team and their skipper, Davis Love III. Initially, there was some trepidation among the event's organizers about whether Poulter, as the scourge of the US side, should share press conferences with some of the players he had vanquished at Medinah, but it was a notion soon squashed by Love himself. "They were a little concerned that they shouldn't put us together because the Ryder Cup was going to come up and I was like 'yes', because Ian is a friend of ours and I'm proud of Ian. That was unbelievable golf [he played]. We're going to go forward as friends and I'll pick on him and he'll pick on me, just like Darren [Clarke] picks on me non-stop about it," he laughs. "It's always going to be that way."

The admiration for Poulter on the other side of the pond wasn't limited to the US skipper, though. Bubba Watson, Ian's fellow rabble-rouser on the first tee at Medinah, was about as fulsome in his praise as was possible. "The guy is great for the game of golf," he beamed. "It's amazing watching where his career started and where it is now. It's amazing to listen to him talk about where he picked up range balls – he worked in the pro shop, did everything – and now he's at the Ryder Cup. So I love his passion and I love how passionate he is about winning it."

Perhaps it was the All-American way in which Poulter played the game, with a manic zeal and a chest-beating patriotism, that had endeared him to his trans-Atlantic contemporaries. It was, after all, not that far from the kind of spirited, gritty and aggressive golf played by so many of the United States' Ryder Cup scrappers over the years, with players like Lanny Wadkins, Corey Pavin and Paul Azinger forever displaying what the American military are wont to call "intestinal fortitude" as they routinely destroyed the opposition. Certainly, Poulter's approach to the competition suggested that he viewed the event as something more akin to a Wild West gunfight than a mere golf tournament. "If it makes me a marked man that's fine by me," he shrugged, when asked about his on-course demeanour. "I guess I've had a bull's-eye on my back for a while. I'm tough to play against in match play, that's important. If guys want to beat me, that's fine. I want to beat them just as bad as they want to beat me and I'm not going to roll over. I'm going to go down blazing, it's dead simple."

While the tributes had flooded in Stateside for Poulter, the European camp had long since been smitten, with every member of the team declaring their admiration and respect for him: José-Maria Olazábal, for example, suggested they build a statue of him. "He's Mr Ryder Cup, he thrives on it," explained his team-mate Sergio Garcia. "He's the one player you really want on your team. He will give everything for his team and he somehow always manages to play at an even higher level when it comes to the event."

Rory McIlroy, his playing partner on that pivotal Saturday evening, meanwhile, was positively effusive. "Ian just gets that look in his eye, especially when he makes one of those big putts, and he's fist-pumping, and he'll just look right through you," he explained. "It's just great to see the enthusiasm and the passion that he has for this event, like all of us do. But this event brings the best out of Ian and if it wasn't for him we wouldn't even have had a chance."

In the close-knit world of professional golf, Poulter's achievements were deservedly lauded but in the wider world the recognition was less forthcoming. Take the BBC's prestigious Sports Personality of the Year Award, the poll that Poulter had so openly criticized two years earlier. In any other year, the exploits of the Ryder Cup team could have scooped two or three of the awards on offer that evening. Olazábal, for instance, may have had a chance of winning the Coach of the Year award, while the European Ryder Cup side would almost certainly have won the Team of the Year. As for Poulter, he would surely have made the shortlist of performers in contention for the main prize, and, with a fair wind and a clever campaign that piggybacked on his huge Twitter following, may well have made the top three. Instead, he was a 300:1 outsider.

It's not as though there wasn't a precedent. In 2006, the Ulsterman Darren Clarke had taken second place in the annual poll after his heroics at the Ryder Cup at the K Club, just weeks after the death of his wife Heather, saw thousands of people throw their weight behind his nomination. Clarke narrowly lost out to the royal three-day-eventer, Zara Phillips.

But this, of course, had been the year of the London 2012 Olympic Games, an event so colossal and so popular that it had rendered most other sporting competitions largely irrelevant, including Sports Personality of the Year. As it was, the only golfer to make the final shortlist of 12 – and the only nominee who hadn't been involved in London 2012 – was Poulter's Ryder Cup team-mate and the reigning world number one, Rory McIlroy, and he would finish in a lowly 10th place, with just 1.83 per cent of the vote. Poulter, meanwhile, would have to content himself with a spot on the stage alongside his close friend Justin Rose to be interviewed by the presenter Gary Lineker about Europe's miraculous recovery at Medinah.

While a lack of recognition from the BBC may not have come as much of a surprise, especially given the Corporation's admiration for all things Olympian, Poulter's Medinah heroics had nevertheless gained him a new legion of admirers. This was particularly true in the media (on both sides of the Atlantic), where his antics of old, from the heinous hairstyles to the high-profile sartorial statements, had often appalled sports scribes as much they had appealed. The *Telegraph*'s Matthew Norman was typical, confessing to a "man-crush" on Poulter and arguing that he is "as entertaining on the course – the fist-shaking, the eyeball-bulging, the fashion sense of a colour-blind circus act on LSD – as he is off it."

Certainly, Poulter's passion and the almost single-handed manner in which he had managed to pull Europe out of a dark and cavernous hole had, it seemed, propelled him into sporting superstardom. "I was stunned, overwhelmed by how much of the attention focused on me," he explained. "When you're involved with the team, you are the team and don't want to take anything away from them. But I suppose what happened on Saturday night was a big turning point and that's why there's been so much interest in me. That and the way I responded, I guess."

It wasn't just European golfers and golf fans who were singing Poulter's praises, though. Everywhere he went, from the Bahamas to Lake Nona, he found himself accosted (in the nicest possible way) by people eager to doff their cap to the Brit with the bulldog spirit. Even the abuse via Twitter had ebbed away. Indeed, the Ryder Cup actually worked wonders for Poulter's beloved Twitter figures too. Typically, he would add around 800 new followers on an average day but as the drama unfolded at Medinah, his following almost brought down the social media network. On Friday, there were 12,500 new recruits, followed by another 34,000 on Saturday. Then, on Sunday, after one of the most improbable days in recent sporting history, 111,000 people signed up to Poulter's page.

The messages of support and goodwill would come from far and wide. Scores of high-profile sports stars offered their congratulations. From footballers to Olympians and Formula One drivers, the great and the good were queuing up to pay homage. "I had so many messages to get through it was unbelievable," said Poulter. "It's gratifying that you not only brought pleasure to so many fans but to so many other sportsmen and women. That means a lot."

Poulter's performances in the Ryder Cup were now also drawing comparisons with Europe's other Ryder Cup stalwart, Colin Montgomerie, a player who, like Ian, had found his true calling in the event. Montgomerie, after all, had enjoyed an almost peerless record, with five wins in eight appearances as player and one victory as captain, and, moreover, an unblemished record in the Sunday singles, where he had never been beaten.

But the comparisons were a little incongruous, not least because, Ryder Cup aside, the two players – the two men – couldn't have been more different. Indeed, they were polar opposites. Poulter was the flash, flamboyant dedicated follower of fashion while Montgomerie was the establishment man, the conservative and sometimes curmudgeonly character at the other end of the style spectrum. What made the comparison all the more amusing was that here were two men with a real history, two players who over the previous decade had clashed more than most, their personalities seemingly grating with each other. Whether it was over course design or playing schedules, rarely a year went by without some bone of contention arising.

Of course, the intriguing aspect of such comparisons was, however, that both men had never claimed a major championship. As the winner of a record eight European Tour Order of Merits and with 31 Tour victories to his name, Montgomerie had come close on several occasions to landing one of golf's four biggest titles, most notably when he lost in play-offs at the 1994 US Open and 1995 PGA Championship. But he had never quite managed to get the job done. Yet for Poulter, and for the wider golfing world, it didn't seem to be as much of an issue.

Perhaps Poulter was fortunate in that he was now playing in an era where the absence of a major title on some of his contemporaries' résumés was of more concern and newsworthiness than his own failure to win one. So while players like Lee Westwood and Luke Donald, both ranked number one in the world at some time in the last three years, Sergio Garcia and, latterly, Montgomerie, always seemed to be bombarded with media questions about their missing majors, Poulter still managed to slip under the radar. Of course, that may be because he has never really come close to winning one in the first place, with just six top-10 finishes from more than 40 attempts. His only real chance came at the 2008 Open Championship at Royal Birkdale when he ran Padraig Harrington close, but still ended four shots adrift of the Irishman.

Yes, Poulter has led in majors and demonstrated that he has the golf game to win, but like Westwood and Donald, he has never managed to string those four special rounds together. That said, his performances in the majors of 2012 represented his best ever results in the blue-riband events – he had three top-10 finishes

– and suggests that maybe he is finally getting the hang of major championship tournament play.

Poulter's not insignificant challenge, then, is to reproduce the form and the focus he has in the intense heat of a Ryder Cup battle and somehow channel his formidable match play prowess into those stroke play events that, rightly or wrongly, are the ones by which great players are always judged. "I've told Ian, 'You are built for the Ryder Cup'," explains Davis Love III. "[But] the thing Ian needs is to figure out how to do that in the Masters, just like Monty needed to play in the US majors like he did in the Ryder Cup too."

Of course, Poulter didn't need Love to tell him that. Straight after the Ryder Cup at Medinah, for example, he had convened a summit meeting with his management team, Paul Dunkley and his son James, to discuss that very problem and how he could bring the edge and the ruthlessness of his Ryder Cup game into the realms of his day job. "We talked about how I could convert that 'killer instinct' I have in the Ryder Cup and in match play events into stroke play competition," he explained.

While time is still on his side to claim a major and, clearly, he's not yet in that dreaded category of being the best player never to have won one (like Montgomerie was seemingly in perpetuity), it is something he is keen to put right at the earliest opportunity. As he explained to the *Guardian* in 2013: "You can't fist pump on the first hole of a stroke play event like you do in the Ryder Cup, it's just not possible. Guys are going to look at you like you've gone completely bonkers if you do that. I guess I am going to have to continue to work on what is going to make me into that player that can play like that for 25 weeks a year. It's about me working in my own brain to get myself revved up as much as I do in the Ryder Cup but do it from within. So it's a complete mindset change and something that I am going to have to think about and continue to work on."

Recent evidence suggests he is getting there. After his fourth place at the BMW Masters in Shanghai, Poulter had teed it up at the WGC-HSBC Champions event in Shenzhen's Mission Hills Golf Club the following week and, although Tiger Woods and Rory McIlroy had given the event a wide berth – McIlroy, for instance, had taken a week off to go and watch his girlfriend, the tennis player Caroline Wozniacki, play in Bulgaria – there were still 13 of the world's top 20 players and 16 men who had taken part at Medinah in attendance.

Two solid but unspectacular opening rounds of 69 and 68 would see Poulter well placed going into the weekend but what happened on Saturday, when he fired an imperious 65, propelled him up the leaderboard and into genuine contention. Come Sunday, and he once more had that undeniable spring in his step and as he moved through the gears, playing almost faultless golf, he arrived at his final hole and promptly hit his approach into the greenside bunker.

It was the manner in which he had extricated himself from a potentially sticky situation, nervelessly splashing out and holing the putt, as though he was just knocking a ball round the garden with the kids, that showed just how confident and at ease he was with his post-Ryder Cup golf game. It would give him his second consecutive round of 65 and a finishing total of 21-under par, two shots clear of a four-man group featuring Ryder Cup stars Jason Dufner and Phil Mickelson, Scott Piercy and the reigning Open champion, Ernie Els.

It would also be Poulter's second WGC victory – the first time an Englishman had achieved that feat – and his weekend total of

14-under-par had seen him overhaul players like Lee Westwood, who had posted a 61 in the third round and the South African Louis Oosthuizen, who had shot a 63 on the Friday. It was proof that, when tested, Poulter could still turn it on in the stroke play events but still there was a distinct feeling that something just wasn't right, and even the winner's cheque for $1.2 million didn't seem to get his blood pumping. Well, maybe it did a little bit. "It still doesn't give you the kind of same buzz you get playing the Ryder Cup," said Poulter afterwards. "There's just not quite as much adrenalin in the body."

Meanwhile in Bulgaria, Rory McIlroy had watched his Ryder Cup partner close out another famous victory and taken to the modern professional's preferred communication tool, Twitter, to send his congratulations. "Ballsy up and down at the last," said the world number one. "Wouldn't expect anything less."

Epilogue

"There is nothing I regret, not even a single pair of trousers. Everything I've done has been for a reason and has served a purpose. You should never look back. There's not enough time to dwell on things in this game. You just have to move on. It'll eat you up otherwise."

When I set out to write this book I thought long and hard about the possible titles we could use for it. There were a few on the table, some good and some not so. *Great Strides* was one that worked on a couple of levels while *All Mouth & Trousers* was another that seemed to fit the bill. And given Poulter's obsession with cars I also thought about calling it *Driven* until someone better read than me pointed out that Nick Faldo had already used that title for his autobiography.

But the fact is that titles like that would have downplayed what is a remarkable story and one that's not so much a rags-to-riches tale as a rag-trade-to-riches one. And it's a story I've wanted to write for a while, even before Poulter became the Ryder Cup superstar we all know and love today.

A few years ago I had been involved in advanced discussions to ghost write his autobiography. We had generous offers from publishers and it had seemed like the project was all good to go. Ultimately, though, Poulter and his agent in the United States, RJ Nemer, had decided that the timing wasn't quite right for him and that, for the time being at least, he wanted to concentrate on his golf and, in all likelihood, try to get the house he had been building finally finished for his family.

In retrospect, it was a good call on his part. Poulter, after all, was at that delicate stage of his career where the money was rolling in and the living was easy, but where there were still questions over his right to be classed as one of the game's very best players. Of course, the 2012 Ryder Cup and the "Miracle of Medinah" would change everything. His performance there, where he almost single-handedly kept Europe in the match before helping them to an improbable and breathtaking victory not only reinforced the views of those who always knew that underneath the neatly pressed shirts and sometimes questionable trousers was a player blessed with a rare belief and talent, but also silenced once and for all the doubters who had him down as little more than a clothes horse on a golf course.

Yes, Poulter enjoys his boys' toys, his expensive cars and his playthings and yes, there's more than a bit of nouveau riche about him, but strip away the layers, the fancy togs and the hair dye and there's a man who has been driven beyond almost all belief, a man who took what was, initially at least, an unremarkable talent and worked on it to such an extent that he made something truly extraordinary out of it. Say what you like about the guy, but don't ever say he doesn't deserve his success.

Now, I've no idea if Ian Poulter will choose to read this book but I doubt it. After all, he's on record as saying that he has only ever read one book in his life and that was Thomas Hauser's biography of Muhammad Ali.

Maybe I should tweet the chapters instead and post them 140 characters at a time...

Index

Index

Index

Picture Credits